LEARNINGEXPRESS

VOCABULARY & SPELLING

in 20 Minutes a Day

Judith N. Meyers

LEARNINGEXPRESS

NEW YORK

Library of Congress Cataloging-in-Publication Data

Vocabulary and spelling in 20 minutes a day.

    p. cm.
  ISBN 1-57685-041-2
  1. Vocabulary—Problems, exercises, etc.   2. English language—
Orthography and spelling—Problems, exercises, etc.
I. LearningExpress (Organization)
PE1449.V58   1996
428.1—dc20   96-17814
                                                CIP

Printed in the United States of America
9 8 7 6 5 4 3
First Edition

ISBN 1-57685-041-2

For Further Information

For information on LearningExpress, other LearningExpress products, or bulk sales, please call or write to us at:

    LearningExpress™
    900 Broadway
    Suite 604
    New York, NY 10003
    212-995-2566

LearningExpress is an affiliated company of Random House, Inc.

Distributed to the retail trade by Random House, Inc., as agent for LearningExpress, LLC.
Visit LearningExpress on the World Wide Web at www.learnx.com.

ISBN 1-57685-041-2

An Important Note to
Our Library Readers

If You're Taking a Job Entrance or National Standards Exam . . .

You've come to the right place! The 20 lessons in this book are designed to help you prepare for a basic skills exam, especially one that includes spelling or vocabulary questions. You'll learn the meaning and spelling of lots of new words, as well as how to figure out a word that you've never seen before when it pops up on the exam. Many of the exercises are in test format to give you plenty of practice. So come exam day . . . you'll be prepared to score your best.

CONTENTS

HOW TO USE THIS BOOK

Words, words, words! They surround us. They fill our senses by sight and sound as we read, listen, or converse in our daily lives. Most of the time we don't think much about the words we use to express our thoughts or feelings. They are so much a part of the way we live that they become remarkable only when we feel their absence—as when we reach for a word that isn't there or sit painfully trying to remember how a word is spelled.

We are aware of words, too, when we are preparing for exams, such as civil service tests or academic entrance tests, which often include sections devoted to vocabulary and/or spelling.

WHY DO CIVIL SERVICE TESTS MEASURE VOCABULARY?

We use our vocabularies—the words we know and how we use them—to reveal what we know to the world. Other people learn about the way we think from the vocabulary we use. A person with a large vocabulary is thus seen as having the advantage of self-expression. For this reason, test makers try to assess how well you have absorbed the language of your culture and how well you can use the words you know to express yourself. They generally accomplish this by testing your recognition of words that are common to our culture and your knowledge of the ways those words are used.

WHY DO CIVIL SERVICE TESTS MEASURE SPELLING?

Many of us feel that we should have left spelling behind in elementary school with Friday spelling tests. You may be annoyed that again, as an adult, you have to deal with the fact that spelling "counts." Part of the reason that we resent having to deal with spelling—whether for a test or in our jobs or daily lives—is that English-language spelling is often just plain *hard*. Our language is visually confusing and phonetically irregular. Its rules are often broken, and the rules are littered with exceptions. But tests often include spelling because, whether we like it or not, people are judged by the way they spell. Our ability to spell words correctly is like the way we wear our hair or dress—both are part of how we present ourselves to the world. By "grooming" our sentences, making sure we present them in a good light, we are saying to our readers that we care enough about our ideas to make sure they appear in public "properly dressed."

HOW TO USE THIS BOOK TO IMPROVE YOUR VOCABULARY AND SPELLING

Here you are, then, for another try at increasing your vocabulary skills and reviewing the basics of spelling, perhaps for the purpose of taking a test. This book is designed for adult learners who are preparing to take an exam or to improve their skills in these areas for other purposes. It is meant to be a guide that enables a working adult like you to improve your skills by studying for about 20 minutes a day.

To use this book for maximum benefit, do the following:

- **Trash this book!** It is meant to be consumable, not passed down to friends or family. Write in it. Doodle in it. Inhabit it. When you have finished, this book should have your "footprints" all over it. You should have the feeling that you've lived in it for the month you've used it. Of course, if this book *is* meant to be used by others—if it's a library book, for example—then you shouldn't write in it but should write your notes on your own pad of paper.

- **Buy a highlighter pen and some markers.** Use them to fill in the exercise pages and to highlight visual cues from the text.

- **Get a pack of index cards.** Boil down the most important parts of each lesson and put them on the cards. Carry the cards with you to review while riding to work or waiting in line, at lunch or whenever you have an extra minute or two of "down time."

- **Share the fun.** Enlist a friend or relative to be your "study buddy" during the month you work on this book. As you complete each lesson, spend another few minutes working with your study buddy. You'll be surprised how much more you will remember if you have shared what you know with someone else.

- **Maintain a "keeper list"** of words you encounter in the real world—at work, on TV, at home. Add them to the words you learn in these lessons. They will double the benefit you derive from using the book by itself.

The first ten lessons of this book focus on vocabulary. The rest are about spelling and about putting together the meanings of words and their spellings. To get started, do the vocabulary self-assessment on the next page.

VOCABULARY SELF-ASSESSMENT

Each of us has three vocabularies in each language that we speak:

- A **speaking** vocabulary: the words and expressions we use every day to communicate.

- A **listening** vocabulary: words and expressions we have heard but may never have used.

■ A **reading** vocabulary: words and expressions we have encountered in print but have neither heard nor used.

One of the best ways to increase your vocabulary is to make a conscious effort to move words from your listening or reading vocabularies to your speaking vocabulary—the words you can not only understand but also use. To see how you currently use your three vocabularies, take the following self-analysis.

SELF-ANALYSIS

Check below the sentences that describe your own vocabulary habits.

_____ **1.** I feel confident that I express myself clearly in speaking.

_____ **2.** I sometimes feel uncomfortable when I know what I want to say but just can't think of the right word.

_____ **3.** I notice unfamiliar words in print and wonder about their meanings.

_____ **4.** Sometimes I come across unfamiliar words in print and feel that I *should* know them.

_____ **5.** I remember words that I had on vocabulary quizzes and tests at school.

_____ **6.** If I write down new words, I can learn them.

_____ **7.** If I come across an unfamiliar word in print, I will look it up in the dictionary.

_____ **8.** If I come across an unfamiliar word in print, I will ask someone to tell me the meaning.

_____ **9.** If I hear an unfamiliar word in conversation or on TV, I will ask someone to tell me its meaning.

_____ **10.** If I meet an unfamiliar word, I am usually embarrassed to ask for or to look up its meaning.

Your answers to the questions above should give you a good sense of how you feel about and use your vocabulary.

There are three ways we learn vocabulary:

■ From the **sound** of words
■ From the **structure** of words
■ From **context,** how the word is **used**

Learning and remembering words, then, is a three-step process:

1. Ask yourself, "Does this word **sound** like anything I've ever heard?" If not, ask:
2. "Does any part of the word **look** familiar?" If not, then ask:
3. "How is this word **used** in the sentence I read or heard?"

Each lesson of this book presents a word list for you to use this process on. First, you can see if you know the words by sight or by sound. Then you'll be given the words in the context of a sentence or paragraph to help you guess the meanings. You'll find that you already know some of the words, and the rest you will learn as you proceed through the lesson.

L · E · S · S · O · N

LISTENING TO AND LOOKING AT WORDS

1

LESSON SUMMARY

This lesson shows you how to listen to words, how to sound out unfamiliar words, and how to learn words that don't sound like what they look like.

W e first learned to speak by listening to others speak. We repeated the sounds we heard and gradually associated meaning with the sounds we made. That's why the *sound* of new words is so important in helping us learn them. Later, when we went to school, many of us kept on learning words by sound when we learned phonics. *Phonics* refers to the system of letter sounds that make up words.

For many words, learning the sounds of the letters and then putting them together allows us to "read" what the word "says." Unfortunately, the English language is full of words that don't *sound* the same as they *look*. Some of the simplest examples that come to mind are *Wednesday* (pronounced *Wendsday,* not *Wed-nes-day*), *business* (pronounced *bizness,* not *bus-i-ness*) and *said* (pronounced *sed,* not *say-id*).

So you can't always count on phonics to help you with new words. For instance, the word *hyperbole,* if sounded out phonetically, sounds like *hyperbowl.* Only if you hear the word will you know that it sounds like *high-PER-bowl-ee.*

Here are some strategies for learning unusual, unfamiliar, or unphonetic words:

1. Listen carefully to the sound of the words you hear.

2. Learn to interpret the phonetic spelling of words when you look up their definitions.

3. Learn how to break words into syllables so that you can hear the parts of the word that carry the meaning.

You'll learn steps 1 and 2 in this lesson and step 3 in Lesson 2—and you'll use all three steps throughout this book.

WORKING WITH WORD LIST 1

BY SIGHT

Here is a list of words which would be difficult to sound out by phonics alone because they contain letter combinations that are phonetically irregular. Put a check mark next to each word you can identify by sight.

blasé	**malign**
bourgeois	**naive**
catastrophe	**passé**
chaotic	**potpourri**
cliché	**précis**
debut	**psyche**
ennui ✓	**rendezvous**
epitome ✓	**slough**
feign	**thorough**
gauche	**villain**

Number of words you know by sight: 18

BY SOUND

If you don't recognize a word on sight, the next step is to try to sound it out phonetically. Phonetic spelling is the spelling of a word that reveals its sound, as opposed to the standard spelling of the word. Most dictionaries write the phonetic spelling immediately following the word listing.

Here are some of the most common phonetic symbols that are used in dictionaries to show the sounds of letters or combinations of letters.

- The *schwa* (written like an upside down *e*) signals a neutral vowel that says, "uh."
  Examples:
  Agent uses a schwa in the second syllable: *a-gənt*.
  Sofa also has a schwa sound: *so-fə*.
- The long and short vowel designations: a line over the letter indicates a long vowel (ā, ē, ī, ō, ū); a curve over the letter indicates a short vowel (ă, ĕ, ĭ, ŏ, ŭ).
  Examples:
  Long vowels "say their own names": ā*ble*, ē*agle*, ī*ce*, nō*te*, fū*se*.
  Short vowels have other sounds: ă*pple*, ĕ*gg*, ĭ *gloo*, ŏ*ctopus*, ŭ*mbrella*.

Below are phonetic spellings for the words in this lesson. These spellings don't use the same symbols the dictionary uses; this is a simpler system based on your knowledge of common words. Accented syllables are in capital letters. Put a check mark next to the words you know by sound.

blasé	*blah-ZAY*
bourgeois	*BOOR-zhwah*
catastrophe	*kat-AS-trə-fee*
chaotic	*kay-OT-ik*
cliché	*klee-SHAY*
debut	*day-BYOO*

ennui	*on-WE*
epitome	*e-PIT-ə-mee*
feign	*FANE*
gauche	*GOWSH*
malign	*mə-LINE*
naive	*nah-EVE*
passé	*pass-AY*
potpourri	*poe-poor-EE*
précis	*PRAY-see*
psyche	*SIGH-kee*
rendezvous	*RON-day-voo*
slough	*SLUF*
thorough	*THOR-oh*
villain	*VILL-en*

Number of words you recognize by sound: _____

BY CONTEXT

Except on vocabulary lists, you don't encounter words all by themselves. They are surrounded by other words that provide a *context*. The context gives you clues to the meanings of words. Here's another pass at some of the words in today's list, this time with a written context.

The past twenty years have seen the emergence of a dread new **villain** in the American **psyche.** The rise of the so-called "drug lords" has been seen as being responsible for the **catastrophes** of drug-addicted infants, battle-scarred neighborhoods, and spiraling crime rates. The traffic in dangerous drugs has spread a **malign** spirit over the childhood of inner-city children, whose lives are often compromised by **chaotic** home lives, broken families, and failing systems designed to protect them. Prompted by these outrages, citizens have called for a **thorough** review of statutes that enable the prosecution of distributors and sellers of illegal drugs and have encouraged long sentences for those who contribute to the spread of this terrible **plague** of drug addiction. We cannot **slough** off our responsibilities for curbing these agents of destruction, who represent the **epitome** of danger to our communities. We cannot afford to be **blasé** about this threat.

The rise of the middle class has made **bourgeois** values paramount in most of American society.

The **potpourri** filled the house with a spicy fragrance.

The young women made their society **debut** at the annual Holiday Ball.

Nehru jackets and love beads are **passé** as fashion trends today.

The late afternoon heat filled the students with an uncomfortable sense of **ennui**.

The teenager felt **gauche** in the company of a more sophisticated crowd.

Despite her brave face, she could not **feign** any real pleasure at the outcome of the election.

The freshman Congressman showed how politically **naive** he was when he heeded the advice of the wily senior senator.

The lovers planned a **rendezvous** away from the city and prying eyes.

The news writer came to rely on journalistic **clichés** that weakened the vivid language on which his reputation rested.

Now add the words you know by their sense and their context to the ones you know by sight or sound.

Total number of words you recognize: _____

DEFINITIONS

Below are the meanings of the words in this lesson. See how many you identified correctly.

blasé: apparently uninterested

bourgeois: middle class

catastrophe: a violent upheaval or great misfortune

chaotic: in a state of confusion or uproar

cliché: an outworn or trite expression

debut: a first appearance in society or in a performance

ennui: boredom, feeling of fatigue

epitome: the highest example of something

feign: pretend

gauche: awkward, immature, ill at ease

malign: 1) deliberately evil; 2) to speak evil of another

naive: innocent, without guile

passé: outdated, old fashioned

potpourri: a mixture, usually of exotic spices and other materials, that gives a pleasant scent

précis: a shortened version of an essay or article

psyche: the human soul

rendezvous: a prearranged meeting, often of a secret nature

slough: 1) to shed, as a skin; 2) to ignore

thorough: complete

villain: an evildoer

PRACTICE

Do the first two exercises below. Check your answers against the key at the end of the lesson. If you score 80 percent or better, go right on to the Test Practice section. If you score less than 80 percent on either exercise (two incorrect answers per exercise), do Exercise 3 for additional practice.

Exercise 1

Match the words in the first column with the lettered definitions in the second column.

_____ **1.** villain

_____ **2.** passé

_____ **3.** ennui

_____ **4.** gauche

_____ **5.** chaotic

_____ **6.** rendezvous

_____ **7.** debut

_____ **8.** psyche

_____ **9.** slough

_____ **10.** cliché

a. a secret meeting

b. a first appearance

c. an outworn expression

d. an evildoer

e. middle class

f. awkward, ill at ease

g. to ignore

h. boredom, fatigue

i. in a state of great confusion

j. the human soul

k. old fashioned

Score for Exercise 1: _____

Exercise 2

Fill in the blanks below with the words from this lesson.

11. The candidate did everything he could to _____ his opponent and cast doubt on his character.

12. For the first assignment, the professor demanded that students write a _____ of a lengthy essay.

13. She pretended to be _____ about her upcoming performance, but secretly she was very excited.

14. She tried to _____ ignorance of her friend's whereabouts but eventually had to confess that she know where she had hidden.

15. Beneath her sophisticated appearance, she was basically _____ about the modeling business.

16. He looked like the _____ of a college professor in his tweed jacket and horn-rimmed glasses.

17. Famine has brought _____ to a number of countries.

18. The mayor ordered a _____ review of all union hiring practices.

19. We tend to think of _____ values as being concerned with making money and aspiring to move up in the world.

20. The scent of _____ made the house smell like a garden in the midst of harsh winter weather.

Score for Exercise 2: _____

If you scored at least 80 percent (8 correct answers) on both exercises, skip Exercise 3 and move on to Test Practice. If you scored below 80 percent on either exercise, use Exercise 3 for additional practice.

Exercise 3

Mark the following statements as true or false, according the meaning of the underlined words.

_____**21.** A naive person would be easily influenced by more knowledgeable people.

_____**22.** A feeling of ennui is a feeling of joy and well being.

_____**23.** A gauche person would be valued as a dinner guest.

_____**24.** A thorough cleaning would leave little to be finished up later.

_____**25.** A cliché is an expression you have probably heard before.

_____**26.** A précis gives just the outline or main ideas of a piece of writing.

_____**27.** The most up-to-date fashions would be considered passé.

_____ **28.** If you <u>slough</u> off a problem, you have probably solved it.

_____ **29.** If you <u>malign</u> someone, that person would probably feel complimented.

_____ **30.** Severe flooding in the Midwest would probably be a <u>catastrophe</u> for most farmers there.

Score on Exercise 3: _____

Test Practice
Circle the answer that means the *opposite* of the words in this lesson.

31. passé
    a. adequate
    b. modern
    c. old fashioned
    d. worn out

32. chaotic
    a. confused
    b. fast moving
    c. excusable
    d. orderly

33. thorough
    a. minimal
    b. thoughtful
    c. expensive
    d. complete

34. ennui
    a. joy
    b. tiredness
    c. energy
    d. effort

35. villain
    a. hero
    b evildoer
    c. criminal
    d. soldier

36. gauche
    a. awkward
    b. silly
    c. sophisticated
    d. beautiful

37. feigned
    a. pretended
    b. was genuine
    c. was unconscious
    d. was surprised

38. malign
    a. poisonous
    b. speak ill of
    c. praise
    d. blame

39. naive
    a. innocent
    b. religious
    c. wise
    d. careful

40. bourgeois
    a. management
    b. middle class
    c. criminal
    d. poor

WRAP UP

Choose ten words that are new to your vocabulary or that you think are important to know. Write five of them in sentences below.

_____

_____

_____

_____

_____

Write the other five words and their definitions on index cards. These will be the beginning of your Keeper List from this book. Review your cards when you have a spare minute throughout the day, and try to use the words in conversation or in writing.

You can also add to your store of cards any words of interest that you come across while reading newspapers, books, or magazines or while listening to the radio, television, or personal conversations.

ANSWERS

Exercise 1
1. d
2. k
3. h
4. f
5. i
6. a
7. b
8. j
9. g
10. c

Exercise 2
11. malign
12. précis
13. blasé
14. feign
15. naive
16. epitome
17. catastrophe
18. thorough
19. bourgeois
20. potpourri

Exercise 3
21. true
22. false
23. false
24. true
25. true
26. true
27. false
28. false
29. false
30. true

Test Practice
31. b
32. d
33. a
34. c
35. a
36. c
37. b
38. c
39. c
40. d

L·E·S·S·O·N

DIVIDE AND CONQUER

2

LESSON SUMMARY

In this lesson, you will see how dividing words into syllables can help you recognize words.

hen we were learning to read, most of us learned to sound out words by syllables. *Syllables* are parts of words which carry separate sounds, though those sounds may be comprised of several letters. Every syllable must have a vowel sound. That vowel *sound* may be made up of more than one vowel *letter*. For instance, in the word *arraignment* (pronounced *ar-rain-ment*), the *a* and *i* together make the long *a* sound. (The *g* is silent.)

Breaking words into syllables is one of the best strategies for seeing if a word is in your listening or reading vocabularies. It also helps to divide and conquer longer words.

RULES FOR DIVIDING WORDS INTO SYLLABLES

Here are a couple of quick rules for dividing words by syllables:

1. Divide between double consonants: *ham-mock*.

2. Divide after prefixes and before suffixes: *in-vest-ment*.

If you already have some feel for how the word sounds you can divide it according to the sound of the vowels:

3. Divide after the vowel if it has the long sound: *so-lar*.

4. Divide after the consonant if the vowel sound is short: *pris-on*.

WORKING WITH WORD LIST 2

BY SIGHT AND SOUND

Here are some words that can be sounded out by their syllables. These words come from the fields of law, business, and government and are typical of the words found on tests for jobs in those areas. They also contribute to your ability to understand current events. Put a check mark next to the words you know by sight.

accessory	litigation
affidavit	negligence
amnesty	perpetrator
cartel	probate
currency	prosecution
deposition	recidivism
depreciation	referendum
filibuster	revenue
incumbent	secession
inventory	subsidy

Number of words you know by sight: _____

Now divide all the words into syllables, using the guidelines above.

Number of words you know by sound: _____

BY CONTEXT

Now read the words in context. See how many you know by the way they are used in the paragraph or sentences, and go back to the word list and check off the ones you now recognize.

Prosecutors were clearly concerned by the **recidivism** rate in the state prisons. They had many **affidavits** and **depositions** confirming that too many **perpetrators** of serious crimes were returning to the courts with second and third offenses. They urged the state to call a **referendum** to increase the **subsidy** to the prison system that would allow more **revenue** to support the costs of keeping criminals in jail. Many applauded these efforts to reduce the incidence of "turnstile justice."

The legislature passed the measure in spite of the long **filibuster** by the downstate lawmaker.

The state legislature refused to consider the **secession** of Staten Island from the City of New York.

The draft dodgers requested **amnesty** from prosecution if they reentered the country.

Incumbent legislators almost always have an advantage over their challengers in elections.

The will was sent to the courts for **probate.**

Our tax laws allow us to account for yearly **depreciation** of some property.

The merchant keeps track of his **inventory** on his computer.

The store was accused of **negligence** because it failed to remove all ice from the sidewalk. It was subsequently involved in lengthy and expensive **litigation.**

Though not involved directly, the man's wife was accused of being an **accessory** in the crime.

Cash **currency** allows for direct sale between two parties.

The oil **cartel** controls the market price of petroleum.

Now add the words you recognize from context to the ones you knew by sight or sound.
Total number of words you know by sight, sound, or context: _____

DEFINITIONS

Here are the words divided into syllables and followed by their meanings:

accessory (*ak-SESS-uh-ree*): one who assists in the commission of a crime

affidavit (*af-fuh-DAY-vit*): a signed statement in a legal proceeding

amnesty (*AM-nes-tee*): general pardon by a government

cartel (*kar-TEL*): an international business association

currency (*KUR-ren-see*): money in circulation

deposition (*dep-uh-ZI-shun*): signed testimony by someone who will not or cannot appear in court

depreciation (*dee-pree-shee-AY-shun*): decline in value

filibuster (*FIL-uh-bus-ter*): a long speech designed to delay legislative action

incumbent (*in-CUM-bent*): currently serving in office

inventory (*IN-ven-to-ree*): goods currently in stock

litigation (*lit-i-GAY-shun*): lawsuits

negligence (*NEG-li-gence*): failure (usually, failure to protect)

perpetrator (*PER-pi-tray-ter*): one who commits a crime

probate (*PROH-bate*): certification of a will

prosecution (*pros-i-KYOO-shun*): the act of bringing an offender before the law

recidivism (*re-CID-uh-viz-um*—note that the *ism* ending is heard as if it had a vowel): repeated criminal behavior

referendum (*ref-uh-REN-dum*): a vote directly by the people

revenue (*REV-uh-noo*): income (often a government's income from taxes)

secession (*se-SESH-un*): a breaking away of one part of a government unit for the purpose of becoming politically independent.

subsidy (*SUB-si-dee*): money given in support of a cause or industry

PRACTICE

Complete the two exercises below. Check your answers with the key at the end of the lesson. If you score below 80 percent on either exercise, do Exercise 3 for more practice.

Exercise 1

Match the words in the first column with their definitions in the second column.

_____ 1. amnesty

_____ 2. currency

_____ 3. probate

_____ 4. referendum

_____ 5. subsidy

_____ 6. revenue

_____ 7. perpetrator

_____ 8. cartel

_____ 9. depreciation

_____ 10. affidavit

a. signed statement in court

b. income

c. international trade association

d. a national business alliance

e. decline in value

f. one who commits a crime

g. financial support

h. money in circulation

i. certification of a will

j. a general pardon

k. a vote by the people

Score on Exercise 1: _____

Exercise 2

Use words from today's list to fill in the blanks below.

11. A lawsuit brought against someone is called _____.

12. A failure to guard adequately against an accident is called _____.

13. A leader currently in office is called a(n) _____.

14. When the same people repeatedly commit crimes, that's called _____.

15. A long speech meant to delay action on a bill in a legislative body is called a _____.

16. The breaking away of one part of a country or community is called _____.

17. A sworn statement by someone who will not be present in court is called a(n) _____.

18. The goods currently stocked by a business are called its _____.

19. One who assists in the commission of a crime is called a(n) _____.

20. The process by which wrongdoers are brought to court is called _____.

Score on Exercise 2: _____

Exercise 3

Mark the following statements as true or false according to the meaning of the underlined words.

_____ **21.** People who receive <u>amnesty</u> are protected from prosecution.

_____ **22.** An <u>incumbent</u> president is a newcomer to the office.

_____ **23.** A sworn statement by someone who is unavailable to the court is an <u>affidavit</u>.

_____ **24.** Taxes contribute <u>revenue</u> to the government.

_____ **25.** <u>Recidivism</u> is the rate of conviction in the court system.

_____ **26.** <u>Depreciation</u> refers to added value of property over a period of time.

_____ **27.** A legislator will <u>filibuster</u> in order to delay action on a bill.

_____ **28.** A <u>referendum</u> is a vote taken in Congress.

_____ **29.** A <u>perpetrator</u> is someone who commits the same crime repeatedly.

_____ **30.** <u>Currency</u> refers to newly printed money.

Score on Exercise 3: _____

WRAP UP

Choose ten words from today's list. Write five of the words in your own sentences below.

_____

_____

_____

_____

_____

Write the other five words and their definitions on your index cards to add to your Keeper List.

ANSWERS

Exercise 1
1. j
2. h
3. i
4. k
5. g
6. b
7. f
8. c
9. e
10. a

Exercise 2
11. litigation
12. negligence
13. incumbent
14. recidivism
15. filibuster
16. secession
17. deposition
18. inventory
19. accessory
20. prosecution

Exercise 3
21. true
22. false
23. false
24. true
25. false
26. false
27. true
28. false
29. false
30. false

L·E·S·S·O·N

COMING UP BY THE ROOTS

3

LESSON SUMMARY

This lesson will show you how to use Greek and Latin roots to build your vocabulary and how to use word structure to help you recognize words.

The first chance you have to understand an unfamiliar word is to "listen" to its sound, as you learned in Lessons 1 and 2. You practiced listening for words in context and dividing words into syllables to sound them out.

Sometimes, however, you can sound out a word and still not understand what it means. The next step, then, is to look at the word's structure. Does the word or a piece of the word sound or look familiar? Sometimes you can connect a part of a word to some other word you already know. It's sort of like meeting someone who reminds you of someone else or meeting a member of a friend's family and recognizing some family characteristic. You may meet words that are not in your listening or reading vocabularies but recognize them as being related to words you do know.

For example, you might come across the word *misanthropic*. You sound it out by syllables—*mis-an-THROP-ik*—but you still don't recognize it. So you look at it again. You see that part of the word is the root *anthro*. You know that the root *anthro* appears in *anthropology*—the study of humankind. Clearly, *anthro* has something to do with being a human. You may also know that the prefix *mis-* generally means *not* or *the opposite of,* as in *misguided*. Without even reading the word in a sentence, you get the idea that *misanthropic* has something to do with *being against or opposed to persons or humanity*. And you're right. A misanthropic person hates society or being in the company of other people.

The pieces of words that carry direct meaning are called the *roots* of the word. Generally roots of English words are derived from ancient Greek and Latin words. Because so many English words have their source in certain recurring root words, knowing some of the most commonly used roots gives you access to many words at once. When you combine your knowledge of roots—the subject of this lesson and the next—with knowledge of *affixes*, small parts that go at the beginning or end of words to change meaning, you have the tools for figuring out the meanings of many words from their structure. Prefixes and suffixes are covered in Lessons 5 and 6.

WORKING WITH WORD LIST 3

BY SIGHT AND SOUND
See how many of the following words you know by sight or sound. You may know the word offhand, or you can look at the highlighted syllable of each word and see if it reminds you of another word you know. Put a check mark next to each word you recognize or can figure out from its root.

ant**agon**ize	*an-TAG-uh-nize*
audible	*AW-duh-bul*
belligerent	*bul-LIJ-er-ent*
chronic	*KRON-ik*
demographic	*dem-uh-GRAF-ik*
fidelity	*fi-DEL-i-tee*
fluctuate	*FLUK-choo-ate*
genocide	*JEN-uh-side*
in**cogn**ito	*in-cog-NEE-toe*
in**duc**ement	*in-DOOS-ment*
interr**rog**ate	*in-TERR-uh-gate*
loquacious	*low-KWAY-shus*
nominal	*NOM-uh-nul*
pathos	*PAY-thus*
pro**tract**ed	*proh-TRAK-ted*
re**ject**ed	*ree-JEK-ted*
sophisticated	*su-FIS-ti-kay-ted*
tenacious	*tuh-NAY-shus*
verify	*VAIR-uh-fie*
vivacious	*vi-VAY-shus*

Number of words you know by sight and sound: ____

If you know another word you think shares the root of one of these words, write that other word next to the word in this list.

BY CONTEXT
Now meet the words in context. See how many you recognize from the way they are used.

One of the most **chronic** problems to face big city politics is the problem of labor relations. Both labor and management tend to become **belligerent** and **antagonize** each other with **vociferous** threats of slowdowns, strikes, work rules, and other methods of **inducement** to get the other side to agree to their demands. Negotiations are often **protracted** and tend to wear down both sides so that they will **reject** efforts that could lead to lasting agreements between the two sides.

Prices may **fluctuate** wildly between one market and another.

The Serb government was accused of attempted **genocide** in its wholesale attacks on the Muslim minority.

Though she was normally **vivacious,** her grief made the woman oddly silent and self-contained.

The actor traveled **incognito** in order to maintain his privacy.

The school charged a **nominal** fee for the use of the gymnasium.

The office tried to **verify** her address so that she could receive her paycheck.

Her **fidelity** to the company was unquestioned despite having offers to go to a competing industry.

The reporter expressed great **pathos** in writing about the tragedy.

Her voice was **audible** from across the room.

Despite her **sophisticated** dress, she was a country girl at heart.

She was **tenacious** in her pursuit of the greatest talent for the show. She wouldn't take no for an answer.

The union **rejected** the offer for a settlement.

The police **interrogated** the prisoner for more than eight hours.

Number of words you recognize by context: _____

DEFINITIONS AND ROOTS

The value of learning roots is that they act as a kind of access key that gives you clues about other words that share the roots or "family lineage " of the word you know.

Below are the definitions and roots of today's 20 words, along with some other words that share their roots. Use these words to complete the exercises below, and watch your word families grow!

antagonize (**agon** = *struggle, contest*): to struggle against
   protagonist, agony, agonize

audible (**aud** = *hear*): able to be heard
   audition, audit, auditorium

belligerent (**bell** = *war*): warlike
   bellicose, antebellum

chronic (**chron** = *time*): occurring over time
   chronological, chronometer, chronicle

demographic (**demo** = *people*): having to do with the measurement of populations
   democracy, demagogue

fidelity (**fid** = *faith*): faithfulness
   Fido, fiduciary, infidel, infidelity

fluctuate (**flux, flu** = *to flow*): to rise and fall
   fluid, fluidity, superfluous, influx

genocide (**gen** = *race or kind*): the deliberate destruction of an entire group of people
   gene, progenitor, progeny

incognito (**cog, gno** = *to know*): unrecognized
   diagnosis, recognize, cognition, cognitive

inducement (**duc** = *to lead*): leading to an action
   induction, reduction, introduction, reduce

interrogate (**rog** = *to ask*): to question
   surrogate, derogatory, arrogant

loquacious (**loc, loq** = *speak*): talkative
   eloquent, soliloquy, epilogue, prologue

nominal (**nom, nym** = *name*): in name only
    nominate, nomenclature, synonym, anonymous

pathos (**path** = *feeling*): feeling of sympathy or pity
    pathetic, empathy, sympathy, pathology, apathy

protracted (**tract** = *draw, pull*): dragged out
    tractor, distracted, attraction, subtracted

rejected (**ject** = *to throw or send*) sent back
    subject, dejected, interjected, projectile

sophisticated (**soph** = *wisdom*): having style or knowledge
    sophomore, sophistry, philosopher

tenacious (**ten** = *hold*): unwilling to let go
    tenacity, contain, tenable

verify (**ver** = *truth*): to establish as truth
    verity, veritable, veracious, aver

vivacious (**viv** = *life*): lively in manner
    vivid, vital, vivisection

PRACTICE

Do Exercises 1 and 2 below. Check your answers against the key at the end of the lesson. If you score at least 80 percent on both exercises, go right ahead to Test Practice. If you score below 80 percent, do Exercise 3 below.

Exercise 1

Match each word in the first column with its definition in the second column.

_____ 1. genocide   **a.** sent back

_____ 2. audible   **b.** feeling of pity

_____ 3. verify   **c.** destruction of a race

_____ 4. tenacious   **d.** in disguise

_____ 5. rejected   **e.** talkative

_____ 6. fidelity   **f.** can be seen

_____ 7. loquacious   **g.** can be heard

_____ 8. antagonize   **h.** faithfulness

_____ 9. incognito   **i.** holding fast

_____10. pathos   **j.** struggle against

                 k. show to be true

Score for Exercise 1: _____

Exercise 2

Complete the sentences below, using words from today's list.

11. The _____ traveler knows the best places to stay.

12. Because he was anxious to rest on the long trip, he shied away from the _____ person in the next seat.

13. The government was eager to _____ the former hostages regarding their experiences.

14. His headaches had caused him _____ pain for many years.

15. The added salary was a(n) _____ to change jobs.

16. The sociologists studied _____ patterns to discover where people were moving in large numbers.

17. Their marriage was strictly _____; they didn't live together but married so the woman could stay in this country.

18. His moods seemed to _____ from happy to sad a great deal of the time.

19. Her _____ manner made her a popular guest at parties.

20. His _____ illness kept him in bed for several months.

Score on Exercise 2: _____

Exercise 3

Mark the following statements as true or false according to the meaning of the underlined word.

_____21. A lack of <u>fidelity</u> in a marriage could lead to divorce.

_____22. A <u>belligerent</u> person would probably be very beautiful.

_____23. Someone traveling <u>incognito</u> would be easily recognized.

_____24. A <u>nominal</u> effort would be rewarded with a large salary.

_____25. A <u>tenacious</u> person would pursue his goals persistently.

_____26. <u>Audible</u> comments would be unable to be heard.

_____27. <u>Chronic</u> behavior happens infrequently.

_____28. <u>Demographic</u> data would serve only one political party.

_____29. <u>Genocide</u> targets only the oldest citizens for destruction.

_____30. It's rarely a good idea to <u>antagonize</u> your boss.

Score on Exercise 3: _____

Test Practice

Choose the word that means the same or almost the same thing as the underlined word in the sentences below:

31. There was an <u>audible</u> sigh of relief when the rescuers brought the drowning man to the surface.
   a. incredible
   b. able to be heard
   c. worthy of praise
   d. able to be seen

32. The lawyer faced his <u>antagonist</u> in the court-room with barely disguised contempt.
   a. opponent
   b. assistant
   c. client
   d. witness

33. Her <u>vivacious</u> manner contrasted with the seriousness of her illness.
   a. grave
   b. hostile
   c. joyous
   d. lively

34. He wanted to <u>verify</u> the ingredients before starting the recipe.
   a. confirm
   b. total
   c. analyze
   d. measure

35. The <u>loquacious</u> dinner guest dominated the conversation.
   a. drunken
   b. talkative
   c. silent
   d. greedy

36. The soap opera emphasized the <u>pathos</u>, rather than the humor, of family life.
   a. sentimental feeling
   b. turmoil
   c. activity
   d. horror

37. He was <u>vociferous</u> in his denial of wrongdoing
   a. outspoken
   b. timid
   c. hostile
   d. brave

38. His <u>chronic</u> lateness was treated with humor by those who had known him for a long time.
   a. occasional
   b. constant
   c. unusual
   d. rare

39. Despite his casual manner, he is a <u>sophisticated</u> man.
   a. hard-working
   b. worldly wise
   c. talented
   d. scholarly

40. He chose to show himself in public <u>incognito</u>, so he could avoid the attention of the press.
- a. in disguise
- b. in casual dress
- c. formally
- d. in person

WRAP UP

Choose ten words from this list. Write five of them in original sentences below. Write the other five on index cards to add to your Keeper List.

_____

_____

_____

_____

_____

ANSWERS

Exercise 1	Exercise 2	Exercise 3	Test Practice
1. c	11. sophisticated	21. true	31. b
2. g	12. loquacious	22. false	32. a
3. k	13. interrogate	23. false	33. d
4. i	14. chronic	24. false	34. a
5. a	15. inducement	25. true	35. b
6. h	16. demographic	26. false	36. a
7. e	17. nominal	27. false	37. a
8. j	18. fluctuate	28. false	38. b
9. d	19. vivacious	29. false	39. b
10. b	20. protracted	30. true	40. a

MORE ROOTING AROUND

4

LESSON SUMMARY
Building on what you learned about roots in Lesson 3, this lesson shows you how to use your knowledge of roots to learn new words.

In Lesson 3, you learned that roots are word elements that share characteristics, much as human beings in families share names and other personal attributes. English words share so many of these traits because they descend from a long line of intermingled languages from the Indo-European family of languages. Many English words come from the Greek and Latin languages, which gave us much of our culture through the ages. Again, the point of learning to recognize roots is that they give you access to whole groups of words when you know a few prolific "families."

Using word elements to increase vocabulary works in two ways:

- You may already know a given root that can guide you in determining the meaning of an unfamiliar word. For example, you may know that the root *hydro* suggests water. Therefore, if you came across the word *hydrotherapy,* you would figure it is a treatment that uses water.
- If you don't know the root by itself, you may recognize it from a word you know. By association, then, you link the known meaning to that of an unfamiliar word. For example, you know that a fire *hydrant*

stores water. Therefore, you associate the root *hydro* to *water* and come up with the meaning of *hydrotherapy*.

WORKING WITH WORD LIST 4

BY SIGHT AND SOUND

Here are some more words that are based on Greek and Latin roots. See how many you recognize either by sight or with the help of the pronunciation guide provided. The roots are highlighted for you.

agora**phob**ic	*ag-uh-ruh-FOH-bik*
as**simil**ate	*uh-SIM-uh-late*
at**trib**ute	*AT-trib-yoot*
benevolent	*buh-NEV-uh-lent*
biodegradable	*by-oh-dee-GRADE-uh-bul*
con**spic**uous	*con-SPIC-yoo-us*
credence	*CREE-dence*
evident	*EV-i-dent*
gregarious	*gre-GAIR-ee-us*
im**ped**iment	*im-PED-uh-ment*
in**cis**ive	*in-SY-siv*
in**fer**ence	*IN-fer-ence*
inter**dict**ion	*in-ter-DIK-shun*
mediocre	*meed-ee-OH-kur*
philanthropy	*fi-LAN-thruh-pee*
pre**ced**ent	*PRESS-i-dent*
re**cap**itulate	*ree-ca-PITCH-yoo-late*
re**mit**tance	*ri-MIT-uns*
tangential	*tan-GEN-shul*
urbane	*ur-BANE*

Number of words you know by sight and sound: _____

BY CONTEXT

Now see how many words you can add to your "known" list when you meet them in context.

It is quite **evident** that we look to television for our awareness of current events. We are drawn to stories served up to us by attractive, **urbane** people whose sophistication gives **credence** to their remarks about a wide range of subjects, though much of television reporting is **mediocre** and offers little more than a mindless **recapitulation** of unimportant facts disguised as news. On occasion, however, reporters offer **incisive** and insightful accounts of world events that enhance our understanding of the events that shape our lives.

The professor was not pleased when the student **contradicted** him in class.

He was **conspicuous** as he drove up in his shiny new car.

She **inferred** from his letters that he was unhappy at school.

His **philanthropy** was well known as his name appeared in association with many charitable causes.

As she grew older she became more **agoraphobic** and refused to leave her home.

The IRS demanded **remittance** of the past due taxes.

His association was merely **tangential** to the larger political party.

His handicap proved to be no **impediment** to his efficiency.

He was a **gregarious** person who loved being with people.

There was no **precedent** to guide the judge's action.

She had many of the **attributes** that he liked in a doctor.

He had failed to **assimilate** to campus life.

The **benevolent** old man gave generously to many worthy causes.

Please use dish detergent that is **biodegradable**.

Number of words you recognize by sound, structure, or context: ____

Look at the word elements in bold print imbedded in the words in Word List 4. Can you think of other words that contain that element? Next to each word write at least one other word you can think of that shares that word element.

DEFINITIONS AND ROOTS

Here are the definitions of the words and the roots contained in the words, along with some additional words that share the roots.

agora**phobic** (**phobe** = *fear*): fear of open spaces
 phobia, claustrophobia, xenophobia
as**simil**ate (**simul** = *copy*): to fit in
 similar, simile, facsimile, simulate
at**trib**ute (**trib** = *to give*): a special quality
 tributary, contribution, tribunal
benevolent (**ben** = *good*): kind
 benefactor, beneficiary, benign, benediction
biodegradable (**bio** = *life*): a living substance able to return to its previous natural form
 bionic, biology, antibiotic

con**spic**uous (**spic** = *see*): highly visible
 spectacle, spectator, inspection, introspection
contra**dict**ion (**contra** = *against*, **dict** = *say*): the act or state of disagreeing
 dictate, dictionary, interdict, dictation
credence (**cred** = *believe*): belief, believability
 creed, credulous, credit, incredible
evi**d**ent (**vid** = *see*): obvious
 video, evidence, visible, provident
gregarious (**greg** = *crowd, herd*): sociable
 egregious
im**ped**iment (**ped, pod** = *foot*; **ped** also means *child*): a barrier or hindrance
 pedestal, pedestrian, pediment
in**cis**ive (**cis, cid** = *to cut*): penetrating, clear cut
 incision, precise, scissors, homicide, suicide
in**fer**ence (**fer** = *bear* or *carry*): an indirect suggestion
 transfer, refer, reference, interfere
mediocre (**med** = *middle*): of medium quality, neither good nor bad
 media, median, intermediate, mediator
philanthropy (**phil** = *love*): giving generously to worthy causes
 philosophy, Philadelphia, bibliophile
pre**ced**ent (**ced** = *go*): a prior ruling or experience
 intercede, procedure, succeed
re**cap**itulate (**cap** = *head*) to review in detail
 capital, caption, captain, decapitate
re**mit**tance (**mit, mis** = *to send*): to pay or send back
 submit, commission, permission, intermission
tangential (**tang, tac, tig** = *touch*): touching slightly
 tangent, tactical, tactile, contiguous
urbane (**urb** = *city*): polished, sophisticated
 urban, suburban, urbanite

PRACTICE

As usual, do Exercises 1 and 2. If you score at least 80 percent on both exercises, go on to the special Bonus Exercise. If you score below 80 percent on either exercise, do Exercise 3 for extra practice.

Exercise 1

Match the word in the first column with its definition in the second column

_____ 1. credence   **a.** obvious

_____ 2. inference   **b.** afraid of cats

_____ 3. mediocre   **c.** a hindrance

_____ 4. gregarious   **d.** kindly

_____ 5. urbane   **e.** of medium quality

_____ 6. agoraphobic   **f.** suggestion

_____ 7. evident   **g.** afraid of open spaces

_____ 8. impediment

     h. sociable

_____ 9. benevolent

     i. believability

_____ 10. conspicuous

     j. sophisticated

     k. stands out visually

Score on Exercise 1: _____

Exercise 2

Fill in the blanks with words from today's list.

11. His remarks were _____ and cut right to the heart of the subject.

12. It doesn't pay to _____ the opinions of those who are in authority.

13. His _____ arose from his deep desire to help those less fortunate than himself.

14. The store demanded the _____ of the payment required to clear the debt.

15. One of her best _____ is her clear-eyed wisdom.

16. Over the years, people from many countries have come to _____ into American life.

17. Public works projects in the 1930s set a _____ for social legislation for the next 60 years.

18. After the game the commentators continued to _____ the key plays for those who had been unable to watch it.

19. She believed that her working life was merely _____ to the "real life" she enjoyed with her family.

20. Scientists need to develop a _____ trash bag that would lessen the problem of waste removal to landfill areas.

Score on Exercise 2: _____

Exercise 3

Answer the following with words from today's list.

21. Which word stems from a root that means *good?* _____

22. Which word stems from a root than can mean *foot* or *child?* _____

23. Which word stems from a root that means to *cut* or *kill?* _____

24. Which word stems from a root that means to *bear* or *carry?* _____

25. Which word stems from a root than means a *fear?* _____

26. Which word stems from a root that means *love?* _____

27. Which word stems from a root that suggests *touching?* _____

28. Which word stems from a root that means *belief?* _____

29. Which word stems form a root that suggests *speaking?* _____

30. Which word stems from a root that suggests *life?* _____

Bonus Exercise: Your Roots are Showing

You can recognize many words from a single root. Complete the paragraph below by writing in as many words as you can; they all stem from the same root.

The root word **cred** means belief. We can see, then, that one's belief system is his **31)** _____. When a storekeeper believes we will pay the bill, she offers us **32)** _____. If we fail to pay those bills, we owe our **33)** _____. If we want to prove that our qualifications can be believed, we offer our **34)** _____. Schools that want their qualifications to be respected want to be **35)** _____. If we are believable, we are **36)** _____. If something is unbelievable, it is **37)** _____. People who believe too easily are **38)** _____.

WRAP UP

Choose ten words from the list that were new or unfamiliar to you before you began today's lesson. Choose five of those ten words and write a sentence for each below.

_____

_____

_____

_____

_____

Write the other five words on index cards and add them to your Keeper List. Ask a friend to quiz you on your Keeper List so far.

ANSWERS

Exercise 1	**Exercise 2**	**Exercise 3**	**Bonus Exercise**
1. i	11. incisive	21. benevolent	31. creed
2. f	12. contradict	22. impediment	32. credit
3. e	13. philanthropy	23. incisive	33. creditors
4. h	14. remittance	24. inference	34. credentials
5. j	15. attributes	25. agoraphobia	35. accredited
6. g	16. assimilate	26. philanthropy	36. credible
7. a	17. precedent	27. tangential	37. incredible
8. c	18. recapitulate	28. credence	38. credulous
9. d	19. tangential	29. contradict	
10. k	20. biodegradable	30. biodegradable	

PREFIXES THAT CHANGE MEANING

5

LESSON SUMMARY

This lesson introduces you to prefixes that affect the meanings of words. By learning some common prefixes, you can learn to recognize many new words.

 refixes are word parts at the beginning of a word that change or add to the meaning of the root word in some way. For example, the Latin root *vert* means to turn. Look what happens when you add different prefixes in front of that root:

- *con* (*with* or *together*) + **vert** = *convert* (*transform*; think *turn together*)

  She wanted to **convert** the old barn into a studio.
- *di* (*two*) + **vert** = *divert* (*turn aside*)

  He wanted to **divert** attention from his shady past.
- *ex* (*out of, away from*) + **vert** = *extrovert* (*an outgoing, out-turning, individual*)

  He was an **extrovert** who was the life of every party.
- *in* (*opposite*) + **vert** = *invert* (*turn over*)

  He inverted the saucer over the cup.
- *intro* (*inside*) + **vert** = *introvert* (*an inwardly directed person*)

  She was an **introvert** who generally shied away from company.
- *re* (*back* or *again*) + **vert** = *revert* (*turn back*)

  He **reverted** to his old ways when he got out of prison.

An acquaintance with the meanings suggested by some of the more common prefixes can help you add to your reading, speaking, and listening vocabularies.

Note that prefixes are often seen in different forms and may fundamentally change the meaning of a root word—making an opposite, for example. Or a prefix may only remotely suggest meaning. **The point of working with prefixes is not to memorize a batch of disconnected word parts but to become familiar with the most common examples**. Then you may be able to figure out how the word meaning may have been affected by a prefix.

WORKING WITH WORD LIST 5

BY SIGHT AND SOUND

The following are words that contain primarily Greek and Latin prefixes. See how many you know by sight or sound. The prefixes are highlighted for you.

antecedent	*an-ti-SEED-ent*
antipathy	*an-TIP-uh-thee*
circumvent	*SIR-kum-vent*
consensus	*kun-SEN-sus*
controversy	*KON-truh-ver-see*
decimate	*DES-uh-mate*
demote	*di-MOTE*
disinterested	*dis-IN-tuh-res-ted*
euphemism	*YOO-fe-miz-um*
exorbitant	*ek-ZOHR-bi-tunt*
illegible	*i-LEJ-uh-bul*
intermittent	*in-ter-MIT-ent*
malevolent	*muh-LEV-uh-lent*
precursor	*pre-KUR-ser*
prognosis	*prog-NO-sis*
retrospect	*RET-roh-spekt*
subordinate	*suh-BOR-din-it*
synthesis	*SIN-thuh-sis*

transcend	*tran-SEND*
trivial	*TRI-vee-ul*

Number of words you know by sight and sound: ____

BY CONTEXT

Now meet each of the words in context. How many do you know when you see how they are used?

Probably no town, city, or state in this country is immune to the **controversy** that always surrounds attempts to cut government budgets. Many communities are already faced with **exorbitant** expenses related to high labor costs, costly social services, and shrinking tax bases. In **retrospect,** we are probably paying for the unprecedented government spending of the last decade. The **consensus** of opinion today, however, seems to be that budgets must be cut, though such cuts threaten to **decimate** the services the neediest people depend on. The **prognosis** for the economic future of our cities, therefore, is guarded.

Her **antecedents** were from Italy.

He tried to **circumvent** the law to avoid paying his parking tickets.

His poor attitude left the manager no choice but to **demote** him.

The Model T was the **precursor** of today's mass produced automobiles.

He often used **euphemisms** to avoid speaking about something distasteful.

His love of his family **transcended** his ambition in business.

When I became a supervisor, I took special training in how to deal with **subordinates.**

She was a **disinterested** person in the negotiations and would not benefit either way.

Her **antipathy** for her former enemy was as strong as ever.

The **intermittent** ringing of the phone kept her awake.

It seemed a **trivial** matter to concern the president of the company.

The writer managed to **synthesize** a number of large ideas into a small, well-written essay.

His **illegible** handwriting made it hard to verify his signature.

The villain had a **malevolent** character that was obvious to all.

Number of words you recognize from context: _____

Now go back to the original list. Look at the prefixes. Write any other words you think you might know that begin with that prefix.

DEFINITIONS AND PREFIXES

Below are the words again with their prefixes and meanings, as well as other words that use the prefix.

antecedents (**ante** = *before*): something that comes before, especially ancestors
  antenatal, antebellum, anteroom

antipathy (**anti** = *against*) hatred, feelings against
  antiwar, antibiotic, antidote

circumvent (**circum, circ** = *around*): to get around
  circumscribe, circulate, circumference

consensus (**con** = *with, together*): agreement on a course of action
  congress, convivial, congregate

controversy (**contr** = *against*): public dispute
  contraceptive, contrast, contrary

decimate (**dec** = *ten*): to destroy or kill a large portion of something
  decimal, decibel

demote (**de** = *down, away from*): to lower in grade or position
  decline, denigrate, deflate

disinterested (**dis** = *not, opposite of*): deriving no benefit from (not the same as *uninterested*)
  disappointed, disabled, disqualified

euphemism (**eu** = *good, well*): a more pleasant term for something distasteful
  euthanasia, euphonious, eugenic

exorbitant (**ex** = *out of, away from*): excessive (literally, out of orbit!)
  exhume, extort, exhale, export

illegible (**il** = *not, opposite*) not readable
  illegal, illegitimate, illicit

intermittent (**inter** = *between*): occurring from time to time, occasional
  intermediate, interlude, intermission, interview

malevolent (**mal** = *bad*): cruel, evil
  malady, malefactor, malice, malignant

precursor (**pre** = *before*): a form that precedes a current model
  premeditate, premature, prevent, preview

prognosis (**pro** = *before*): opinion about the future
state of something
provide, professional, produce

retrospect (**retro** = *back, again*): hindsight
retroactive, retrograde, retrorocket

subordinate (**sub** = *under*): lower in rank
subterranean, substrate, subscription

synthesis (**syn, sym** = *with* or *together*): the combination of many things into one
synthetic, symphony, symbiotic

transcend (**trans** = *across*): to go beyond
transfer, transportation, transatlantic

trivial (**tri** = *three*): unimportant
tripod, triangle, triennial

    Note that some words translate very neatly into
their components:

- **Antipathy** means literally *feelings against* (*anti =
against, path = feelings*).

- **Retrospect** means literally *looking back* (*retro =
back, spect = to look or see*).

    The connection between the meaning of the prefix and the meaning of the word is much less obvious
in other cases. For instance, the word **trivial** comes from
the place where, in ancient times, the three main caravan routes met and people exchanged gossip and bits
of information. Today we use *trivial* to refer to any small
items of information that are relatively unimportant.

PRACTICE

Do the first two exercises below. Check your answers
at the end of the lesson. If you score at least 80 percent
on both exercises, go on to Test Practice. If you score
below 80 percent on either exercise, do Exercise 3 for
additional practice.

Exercise 1

Match each word in the first column with its meaning
in the second column.

_____ 1. antipathy   **a.** hindsight

_____ 2. prognosis   **b.** cruel

_____ 3. exorbitant   **c.** forecast

_____ 4. intermittent   **d.** unreadable

_____ 5. malevolent   **e.** unqualified

_____ 6. retrospect   **f.** hatred

_____ 7. antecedents   **g.** forebears

_____ 8. subordinate   **h.** bring together

_____ 9. synthesize   **i.** lower in rank

_____10. illegible   **j.** recurring

    k. excessive

Exercise 2

Complete each of the sentences below with a word from today's list.

11. The manager threatened to _____ the clerk if he came late one more time.

12. The union leaders finally reached a _____ over the salary package.

13. The Civil War _____ both the land and the population of the South.

14. The jumbo jets were the _____ of today's SSTs.

15. The choice had to be made by a _____ person who would not benefit from the outcome.

16. Using too many _____ to avoid tasteful subjects weakens our ability to express ourselves clearly.

17. The boy always found a way to _____ authority and get his own way.

18. She likes to meditate on the words of the great philosophers in order to _____ her mundane concerns.

19. Many people focus on the _____ things in life and ignore the more important matters.

20. Peace-loving people try to avoid _____ with others.

Exercise 3

Mark the following statements as true or false according to the meaning of the underlined word.

_____21. Most people would want to pay an exorbitant sum for a theater ticket.

_____22. An intermittent action is of short duration.

_____23. A retrospect(ive) exhibition shows only recent works by an artist.

_____24. A disinterested person is bored with her work.

_____25. A consensus opinion represents the group that makes the decision.

_____26. A malevolent character in a movie is usually the hero.

_____27. One's children are one's antecedents.

_____28. Only trivial matters are referred to the CEO of the company.

_____29. If you have antipathy toward someone, you have little or no feeling at all.

_____30. We use euphemisms when we want to soften the meaning of what we say.

Test Practice

Choose the word or phrase that best means the *opposite* of the underlined word below.

31. a <u>synthesis</u> of ideas
    a. blending
    b. review
    c. separation
    d. sharing

32. a <u>decimated</u> area
    a. intact
    b. scenic
    c. damaged
    d. beautiful

33. <u>illegible</u> handwriting
    a. invisible
    b. unqualified
    c. unreadable
    d. clear

34. an <u>exorbitant</u> price
    a. expensive
    b. unexpected
    c. extraordinary
    d. reasonable

35. a <u>subordinate</u> principle
    a. unimportant
    b. underlying
    c. lower
    d. higher

36. one's <u>antecedents</u>
    a. enemies
    b. descendants
    c. forefathers
    d. interests

37. to <u>circumvent</u> the rules
    a. break
    b. follow
    c. change
    d. ignore

38. an <u>intermittent</u> action
    a. uncertain
    b. single
    c. negative
    d. definite

39. a <u>trivial</u> question
    a. significant
    b. petty
    c. worthless
    d. tricky

40. a <u>malevolent</u> spirit
    a. evil
    b. spiteful
    c. mischievous
    d. kindly

WRAP UP

Choose ten words from the list above. Write five of them in sentences below.

Write the other five words on index cards to add to your Keeper List.

_____

_____

_____

_____

_____

ANSWERS

Exercise 1	Exercise 2	Exercise 3	Test Practice
1. f	11. demote	21. false	31. c
2. c	12. consensus	22. true	32. a
3. k	13. decimated	23. false	33. d
4. j	14. precursors	24. false	34. d
5. b	15. disinterested	25. true	35. d
6. a	16. euphemisms	26. false	36. b
7. g	17. circumvent	27. false	37. b
8. i	18. transcend	28. false	38. b
9. h	19. trivial	29. false	39. a
10. d	20. controversy	30. true	40. d

L·E·S·S·O·N 6

SUFFIXES THAT IDENTIFY THE "JOB"

LESSON SUMMARY
This lesson shows you how suffixes change the "work" of a word by signaling parts of speech.

The past three lessons have discussed the pieces of words that carry and change the meaning of the word. This lesson will concentrate on the word endings—*suffixes*—that signal how a word is being used in a sentence.

You may remember from school days that words are divided into something called the "parts of speech"—primarily nouns, which name something; verbs, which are action or existence words; and adjectives and adverbs, which describe other words. Suffixes often change the part of speech of a word.

For example, take the word *devote,* meaning *to dedicate time to the care of* someone or something. Suffixes change the way the word works in a sentence.

- As a **verb,** it appears as it is:
  I will *devote* my time to my family.
- As a **noun,** it "wears" the *-tion* suffix and becomes *devotion*:
  His *devotion* to his family was well known.
- As an **adjective** modifying a noun it wears the *-ed* suffix:
  He is a *devoted* family man.
- As an **adverb** modifying a verb it wears the *-ly* suffix:
  He served his family *devotedly* for many years.

Thus, adding a suffix often changes the function of the word in a sentence without fundamentally changing the word's meaning. You can think of a suffix as the "outfit" or uniform a word wears for a particular job in the sentence, just as you may wear different outfits for different activities: a suit or uniform for work, jeans for household chores, and a track suit jogging.

WORKING WITH WORD LIST 6

BY SIGHT AND SOUND

The 20 words below contain suffixes that identify the word as working at a particular job in the sentence. As you look at the words and determine whether you know them by sight or sound, think about words you already know that contain the same suffix. Let what you already know help you figure out the meanings of words which may be new to you.

agrarian	*uh-GRARE-ee-an*
bigotry	*BIG-uh-tree*

consummate	*KON-suh-mate*
copious	*COPE-ee-us*
cryptic	*KRIP-tik*
deferment	*di-FER-ment*
etymology	*et-uh-MOL-uh-jee*
furtive	*FUR-tiv*
laudable	*LAW-duh-bul*
mutation	*myoo-TAY-shun*
obsolescence	*ob-suh-LESS-ence*
parity	*PAIR-i-tee*
pragmatism	*PRAG-muh-tiz-um*
protagonist	*proh-TAG-uh-nist*
provocative	*pruh-VOK-uh-tiv*
puerile	*PYOO-ruh-ul*
rectify	*REK-ti-fie*
relentless	*ri-LENT-less*
satirize	*SAT-uh-rize*
venerate	*VEN-uh-rate*

Number you know from sight and sound: _____

For Non-Native Speakers of English (and Others)

Note that words often have more than one meaning and can do more than one "job." For example, the word *root* is used in this book to mean *a part of a word that carries meaning*. But the word *root* has other meanings:

- As a noun it can mean:
  the part of a plant that is underground. Pull that plant out by the root.
  the base of the hair shaft. Her roots showed she needed a new dye job.

- As a verb it can mean:
  to undertake a search. They rooted around the room looking for the missing ring.
  to cheer for. They rooted for the winning team.

For sharp eyes only: Turn to the first paragraph in Lesson 4. Circle three words in that paragraph that contain roots, prefixes, and/or suffixes contained in these lessons. Find two root words in Lesson 6 that you recognize from your work so far.

BY CONTEXT

Now meet the words in context. See how many more you know from their uses in sentences.

One of the most **provocative** employment issues today is that of minority hiring in major industries. In an effort to **rectify** discrimination caused by past **bigotry** and to offer **parity** with other workers, some industries are offering special incentives for minority workers. Though these motives are **laudable** in many ways, these actions will doubtless meet with **relentless** resistance from those who feel that any kind of favoritism is unfair.

He seemed to behave in a **furtive**, almost secretive, manner.

He tried to get a **deferment** that would allow him to delay his induction into the army.

She made a **cryptic** comment that was difficult to interpret.

The **protagonist** in the play suffered many misfortunes.

His **pragmatism** allowed him to make realistic decisions.

The **agrarian** way of life has gradually given way to a more urban society.

David Letterman likes to **satirize** political life.

His **puerile** behavior made him seem childish and immature.

He took **copious** notes before the final exam.

It is interesting to know the **etymology** of unfamiliar words.

The sales director wanted to **consummate** the transaction before another vendor made a bid.

The automotive industry builds a certain amount of **obsolescence** into cars so that they will need to be replaced in a few years.

In some parts of the world people **venerate** their elders.

Many organisms are known for their **mutations,** which allow them to change form over the course of their lifetimes.

Number of words you know from context: _____

DEFINITIONS

Here are the definitions of the words in today's list. Do they mean what you thought they did?

agrarian: having to do with agriculture or farming
　The farmer loved his **agrarian** life.
bigotry: intolerance
　We must guard against **bigotry** wherever it exists.
consummate: to make complete
　The deal was **consummated** after long negotiations.
copious: plentiful
　He shed **copious** tears over the tragic bombing in Oklahoma.
cryptic: mysterious, hidden
　She made a **cryptic** comment that was unclear to everyone.
deferment: delay
　He wanted a **deferment** on paying his student loans.

etymology: study of word origins

The scholar was an authority on the **etymology** of words.

furtive: underhanded and sly

He had a **furtive** manner.

laudable: praiseworthy

He had **laudable** intentions to do good in his community.

mutation: a change in form

The scientist found a significant **mutation** in the gene.

obsolescence: the state of being outdated

The new designs were already headed for **obsolescence.**

parity: equality

He wanted **parity** with the other employees.

pragmatism: faith in the practical approach

His **pragmatism** helped him run a successful business.

protagonist: one who is the central figure in a drama

The **protagonist** was played by a great actor.

provocative: inciting to action

The actions of a few demonstrators were **provocative.**

puerile: childish

The father's actions were **puerile**; his five-year-old was more mature.

rectify: to correct

He wanted to **rectify** the misunderstanding.

relentless: unstoppable

He was **relentless** in his search for knowledge.

satirize: to use humor to expose folly in institutions or people

Comedians like to **satirize** politicians.

venerate: to respect or worship

He **venerated** his parents and protected their interests.

SUFFIXES

The table on the next page shows suffixes used in Word List 6. They are divided into the parts of speech or the "jobs" they suggest for the words. Other words which contain those suffixes are listed. In the last column, add at least one other word that uses the suffix, besides the ones in today's word list.

PRACTICE

Complete Exercises 1 and 2 and then check your answers at the end of the lesson. If you score below 80 percent on either exercise, do Exercise 3 for additional practice.

Exercise 1

Match the word in the first column with its meaning in the second column.

_____ 1. pragmatism   **a.** praiseworthy

_____ 2. bigotry   **b.** respect

_____ 3. puerile   **c.** plentiful

_____ 4. copious   **d.** mysterious

_____ 5. consummate   **e.** realism

_____ 6. rectify   **f.** intolerance

_____ 7. cryptic   **g.** underhanded

_____ 8. venerate   **h.** practicality

_____ 9. laudable   **i.** childish

_____10. furtive   **j.** complete

   k. correct

Score on Exercise 1: _____

NOUN ENDINGS

Suffix	Meaning	Examples	Your Example
-tion	act or state of	retraction, contraction	
-ment	quality of	deportment, impediment	
-ist	one who	anarchist, feminist	
-ism	doctrine of	barbarism, materialism	
-ity	state of being	futility, civility	
-ology	study of	biology, psychology	
-escense	state of	adolescence, convolescence	
-y, -ry	state of	mimicry, trickery	

ADJECTIVE ENDINGS

Suffix	Meaning	Examples	Your Example
-ic	causing, making	nostalgic, fatalistic	
-ian	one who is or does	tactician, patrician	
-ile	pertaining to	senile, servile	
-ive	having the nature of	sensitive, divisive	
-less	without	guileless, reckless	

VERB ENDINGS

Suffix	Meaning	Examples	Your Example
-ize	to bring about	colonize, plagiarize	
-ate	to make	decimate, tolerate	
-ify	to make	beautify, electrify	

Exercise 2

Mark the following statements as true or false according to the meanings of the underlined words.

_____11. A <u>deferment</u> allows immediate action.

_____12. The <u>protagonist</u> is usually the most important person in a play.

_____13. Most people think that wage <u>parity</u> is a good idea, at least in theory.

_____14. <u>Obsolescence</u> adds value to merchandise.

_____15. <u>Etymology</u> is the study of insect life.

_____16. A <u>mutation</u> can be a change of form.

_____17. A <u>relentless</u> search is over quickly.

_____18. <u>Provocative</u> comments are usually comical.

_____19. A <u>furtive</u> glance is sly and secretive.

_____20. <u>Agrarian</u> life is found in the city.

Score on Exercise 2: _____

Exercise 3

Complete the following sentences.

21. If you <u>venerate</u> something, you

_____.

22. If you request at <u>deferment</u>, you want

_____.

23. If you want to <u>rectify</u> a situation, you must

_____.

24. If you are a <u>relentless</u> person, you

_____.

25. If your motives are <u>laudable</u>, they are

_____.

26. If you <u>satirize</u> something, you

_____.

27. If you behave in a <u>puerile</u> manner, you are

_____.

28. If you behave in a <u>furtive</u> way, you are being

_____.

29. If you want <u>parity</u> at work, you want

_____.

30. If you <u>consummate</u> arrangements for a trip,

you _____.

Score on Exercise 3: _____

WRAP UP

Choose ten words from today's list that you want to learn. Write five of them in sentences below.

_____

_____

_____

_____

_____

Write the other five words on index cards to add to your Keeper List. You should now have 30 or more words on your Keeper List. Ask someone to quiz you on their definitions.

ANSWERS

Exercise 1	**Exercise 2**	**Exercise 3**
1. e	11. false	21. respect it
2. f	12. true	22. a postponement
3. i	13. true	23. correct it
4. c	14. false	24. don't give up
5. j	15. false	25. praiseworthy
6. k	16. true	26. make fun of it
7. d	17. false	27. childish
8. b	18. false	28. sly and sneaky
9. a	19. true	29. equal treatment
10. g	20. false	30. finalize them

L·E·S·S·O·N 7

USING CONTEXT CLUES TO "PSYCH OUT" MEANINGS

LESSON SUMMARY

Today's lesson focuses on using context to understand the meanings of words. Two kinds of context clues are covered: definition and contrast. Two additional types will be covered in Lesson 8. Today's vocabulary list presents words that come from other languages.

essons 1–6 concentrated on figuring out the meaning of unfamiliar words by decoding and analyzing the words themselves. The concept of *context*—the words and sentences around an unfamiliar word—should already be familiar to you. This lesson and the next will focus more specifically on context, showing you how to use context to get "clues" about the meanings of words.

There are basically four kinds of context clues:

1. Context clues by **definition**, in which the writer defines the word in the sentence.

2. Context clues by **contrast**, in which words are presented as the opposite of the meaning conveyed by the surrounding text.

3. Context clues by **example**, in which the writer offers an illustration of the meaning of the word.

4. Context clues by **restatement**, in which the author follows the sentence with a clarifying sentence.

The first two kinds of context clues are covered in this lesson and the other two in Lesson 8.

WORKING WITH WORD LIST 7

As you saw in Lesson 1, many words in the English language come directly from foreign languages, with their original pronunciation and meaning intact. To understand these words, you usually have to rely on your listening skills or use the context, because usually they are difficult to sound out phonetically.

BY SIGHT AND SOUND

In the words that follow, the pronunciation and the source language are provided for you. Unless you recognize the word meaning by sight or sound, you'll have to rely on the context to determine the meaning.

aficionado (Spanish)	*uh-FIS-ee-uh-NA-doe*
apartheid (Afrikaans)	*a-PART-hate*
carte blanche (French)	*kart BLAHNCH*
caveat (Latin)	*KAH-vee-at*
charisma (Italian)	*ka-RIZ-ma*
chutzpah (Yiddish)	*HOOTS-pah*
coterie (French)	*KOH-tuh-ree*
coup d'etat (French)	*koo day-TAH*
detente (French)	*day-TAHNT*
dilettante (Italian)	*dil-e-TANT*
ersatz (German)	*ER-zatz*
faux pas (French)	*foe PAH*
junta (Spanish)	*HOON-tah*
kibitz (Yiddish)	*KIB-itz*
malaise (French)	*mal-AYZ*
naivete (French)	*nah-eev-TAY*
pariah (Hindi)	*puh-RY-uh*

peccadillo (Spanish)	*pek-uh-DIL-oh*
pundit (Hindi)	*PUN-dit*
repertoire (French)	*REP-er-twar*

Number of words you know by sight and sound: _____

BY CONTEXT
Definition Clues

In the sentences that follow, the words from today's list are defined directly in the sentence. These are *context clues by definition*. Take the following sentence as an example: *His entourage, that is, his train of helpers, followed him everywhere.* In this sentence, *train of helpers* defines *entourage*, and the phrase *that is* even tells you in advance that a definition is coming up.

Circle the definition embedded in each sentence; you'll see that the definition lets you know what each word means.

He was known as a **pundit**, an expert, on etymology.

The commission issued a **caveat**, warning against employees' "double dipping" from the city's treasury.

Only he would have the **chutzpah**, the nerve, to ask her for a ride after insulting her.

He had a wide **repertoire,** or collection, of musical works to draw on.

After his release from prison the man remained a **pariah**, an outcast in the community.

After the revolution, power in the country was assumed by the **junta,** the group that seized power by force.

The candidate had a certain **charisma**, a forceful personality that made people want to follow him.

He was rarely seen without his **coterie,** the group of friends he considered to be loyal to him.

After the war he sank into a **malaise,** a sadness he just couldn't overcome.

He was an **aficionado**, a devoted fan, of professional boxing.

Contrast Clues

In the next set of sentences the words appear with context clues by contrast. A contrast clue *sets the word against its opposite* Here's an example: *Though he said his art was avant garde, it really seemed rather old fashioned.* In contrast to *old fashioned, avant garde* means *brand new* or *ahead of the times.*

Circle the context clue in each of the following sentences:

Though he professed to be on a budget, he seemed to have **carte blanche** to buy whatever he wanted.

He said the bag was genuine kidskin, but I knew that it was merely **ersatz** leather.

Though her appearance was sophisticated, her manner showed her real **naivete.**

Though he tried to dismiss his actions as harmless **peccadillos**, I believed that more serious crimes were involved.

He regarded himself as a professional, but I thought he was merely a **dilettante**.

Though both parties said they could not agree, they managed to arrive at a **detente**.

She said she minded her own business, but actually she loved to **kibitz** with anyone she could find.

They said that racial integration had been achieved, but we knew that **apartheid** still existed in South Africa for many years.

Though he generally had good social skills, he nonetheless was remembered for his embarrassing **faux pas.**

Using the definition and contrast clues, write your own definition next to each word on Word List 7.

Number of words you know by sight, sound, and context: _____

For Non-Native Speakers (and Others)

Watch for ways that punctuation helps to find context aids. Here are some ways punctuation is used to clarify word meaning in sentences:

- **Definitions are often set off with commas:** He was an aficionado, a devoted fan, of the Dallas Cowboys.
- **Examples are often set off by a semicolon and a comma:** He issued a caveat; that is, he warned the employee that he had to come on time or be fired.
- **Contrasts are often introduced by a comma:** Though he demanded carte blanche to do his own stunts in the movie, the director still limited his action sequences.

DEFINITIONS

Here are the definitions of the words on List 7. Compare them with the definitions you wrote above.

aficionado: a devoted fan
apartheid: official separation of races
carte blanche: unlimited authority
caveat: a warning
charisma: compelling personality
chutzpah: nerve, gall
coterie: a group of followers
coup d'etat: a sudden overthrow of power
detente: an agreement
dilettante: a dabbler
ersatz: synthetic, fake
faux pas: a social error
junta: a group that seizes power
kibitz: meddle
malaise: a feeling of sadness or lethargy
naivete: innocence, simplicity
pariah: an outcast
peccadillo: misdemeanor, small sin or fault
pundit: expert, authority
repertoire: a list of someone's works or skills

PRACTICE

Complete Exercises 1 and 2 below. Check your answers using the key at the end of the lesson. If you score 80 percent or more on both exercises, go on to Test Practice. If you score below 80 percent on either test, do Exercise 3 for more practice.

Exercise 1

Match the words in the first column with their meanings in the second column:

_____ 1. repertoire

_____ 2. coterie

_____ 3. dilettante

_____ 4. kibitz

_____ 5. faux pas

_____ 6. junta

_____ 7. aficionado

_____ 8. pariah

_____ 9. pundit

_____ 10. naivete

a. a social error

b. a dabbler in the arts

c. an expert or authority

d. a devoted fan

e. to gossip

f. favorable character

g. innocence, lack of sophistication

h. a group that takes power

i. a loyal following

j. an outcast

k. a list of talents or works

Score on Exercise 1: _____

Exercise 2

Next to each sentence, write D if the sentence gives a context clue by definition or C if the context clue is by contrast.

_____11. He offered a *caveat*, a warning, about the dangers of smoking.

_____12. Though he tried to appear energetic, we all knew that he suffered from a *malaise*.

_____13. The coffee, though we knew it was *ersatz*, tasted genuine.

_____14. She had a charming *naivete*, or lack of sophistication.

_____15. As a youth he had committed a harmless *peccadillo*, hardly a serious crime.

_____16. They reached a *detente*, or agreement, after all the negotiations were complete.

_____17. She liked nothing better than to *kibitz* around the neighborhood, meddling in everyone's business.

_____18. *Apartheid*, the official separation of the races in South Africa, is now illegal.

_____19. He was embarrassed that his *faux pas*, a small social misstep, had created so much fuss.

_____20. He claimed that the *coup d'etat*, the sudden overthrow of power in the small country, was successful.

Score on Exercise 2: _____

Exercise 3

Mark the following sentences as true or false according to the meaning of the underlined words.

_____21. A <u>faux pas</u> could cause social embarrassment.

_____22. A <u>dilettante</u> is a seasoned professional.

_____23. An <u>aficionado</u> of baseball might join the <u>coterie</u> around a famous player.

_____24. A person with <u>charisma</u> would be an effective leader.

_____25. Someone with <u>chutzpah</u> could appear to be rude and thoughtless.

_____26. A <u>pariah</u> would be welcome in anyone's home.

_____27. A <u>pundit</u> is a humorous speaker.

_____28. A new bride would love an <u>ersatz</u> diamond.

_____29. A <u>junta</u> is usually elected by the people.

_____30. A <u>coup d'etat</u> takes place slowly over a period of time.

Score on Exercise 3: _____

Test Practice

Circle the word that best completes each of the following sentences.

31. His (charisma/chutzpah) made him a natural leader.

32. He remained a (dilettante/detente) despite his years of training in art.

33. He always felt that he was a (peccadillo/pariah) among the smart set.

34. He committed a (faux pas/malaise) that no one ever forgot.

35. His (repertoire/coterie) included many old favorites.

36. There was a major (caveat/coup d'etat) in the small country over the weekend.

37. The fact that he was a well known (aficionado/pundit) was no surprise to those who knew of his superior knowledge.

38. He made fun of the child's (naivete/ersatz).

39. The general formed a (junta/kibitz) to overthrow the government.

40. The policy of (apartheid/carte blanche) has led to great tragedy over the years.

WRAP UP

Choose ten words from Word List 7. Use five of the words to write sentences below. Include as many context clues, by definition or by contrast, as you can. Then write the remaining five words on index cards and add them to your Keeper List.

_____

_____

_____

_____

_____

ANSWERS

Exercise 1	Exercise 2	Exercise 3	Test Practice
1. k	11. D	21. true	31. charisma
2. i	12. C	22. false	32. dilettante
3. b	13. C	23. true	33. pariah
4. e	14. D	24. true	34. faux pas
5. a	15. C	25. true	35. repertoire
6. h	16. D	26. false	36. coup d'etat
7. d	17. D	27. false	37. pundit
8. j	18. D	28. false	38. naivete
9. c	19. D	29. false	39. junta
10. g	20. D	30. false	40. apartheid

L·E·S·S·O·N

MORE CONTEXT CLUES 8

LESSON SUMMARY

This lesson focuses on two kinds of context clues: examples and restatements. The Word List presents words that come from the names of people, places, or events. Context is often the best way to determine the meanings of such words.

By now you have noticed a number of facts about the English language:

- It is visually confusing and phonetically irregular.
- Words have different forms for different purposes—the parts of speech.
- Words often share elements that help to signal meaning—roots and affixes.
- Sometimes word meaning is clear only from context.
- Some words come into the language directly from other languages.

The difficulty of the English language lies partly with its complexity. The delight of the English language is its ability to grow and adopt new words from many sources. In this lesson and in Lessons 9 and 10—the last vocabulary lessons before we turn to spelling—you will see how new words come into the language from such sources as place names, personal names, historic or literary references, and new technology.

This lesson also focuses on two additional kinds of context clues that help you determine what a word means: context clues by **example** and context clues by **restatement**. These kinds of clues are particularly helpful with words that have been derived from names and with newly created technological words, because many such words do not have phonetic or structural clues to help you determine meaning.

WORKING WITH WORD LIST 8

Word List 8 contains words that are drawn from names of people or places, some real and some fictional. The meanings of the words come from some association with the name. For example, the word *boycott,* which means a refusal to buy something or pay for something, comes from the name of an Irish landlord whose harsh policies led his tenants to refuse to pay his rents.

BY SIGHT AND SOUND

Read the list and see how many words you recognize by sight or sound.

bedlam	*BED-lum*
chauvinistic	*show-vuh-NIS-tik*
cynical	*SIN-i-kul*
draconian	*dra-KOH-nee-un*
erotic	*e-ROT-ik*
forensic	*fuh-REN-sik*
gerrymander	*JER-ee-man-der*
jovial	*JO-vee-al*
masochist	*MAS-uh-kist*
maudlin	*MAWD-lin*
maverick	*MAV-er-ik*
mecca	*MEK-uh*
mentor	*MEN-tor*
mesmerize	*MEZ-mer-ize*

narcissistic	*nar-si-SIS-tik*
quixotic	*kwik-SOT-ik*
stoic	*STOW-ik*
tantalize	*TAN-tuh-lize*
titanic	*tie-TAN-ik*
utopia	*yoo-TOE-pee-uh*

Number of words you know by sight and sound: _____

BY CONTEXT
Example Clues

Ten of today's words are presented below with context clues by example. In the following sentences, the writer uses an example to illustrate word meaning. Circle the examples that help you figure out what the words mean.

The harsh and punishing laws passed by this legislature were truly **draconian** in nature.

The magician kept every eye on his spellbinding performance, which was completely **mesmerizing** to the audience.

Broadway is the **mecca** of the musical theater and draws performers from all over the world.

The candidate tried to envision a **utopian** society in which all social problems had been solved.

His **stoic** manner in his last illness won the respect of everyone in the hospital.

His outrageous opinion on the place of women in society suggested unbridled **chauvinism.**

His experience with government corruption had made him **cynical** about the motives of others.

His concern with his personal appearance and pre-occupation with his own problems made him seem too **narcissistic** for her taste.

The boss's **tantalizing** promise of a promotion made her decide to stay at her job.

He seemed to take an almost **masochistic** pleasure in reliving his horrible experience.

Restatement Clues

Here are the other ten words in sentences that contain context clues by restatement. In the following sentences, the writer has clarified the meaning of an unfamiliar word by writing a sentence or phrase to illustrate it.

He was considered a real **maverick** in the Congress. He refused to follow his party's platform on nearly every issue.

He threatened to **gerrymander** the district. His redrawing of election lines to favor his candidate would have meant defeat to the other party.

She was a **jovial** hostess. She was always in the midst of the group with a humorous story or joke to raise everyone's spirits.

Unfortunately she became **maudlin** when she drank too much. She would weep and tell long sentimental stories of her unhappy childhood.

He honed his **forensic** skills in college. He participated on the debate team and was speaker at his commencement ceremony.

He mounted a **quixotic** campaign. He pursued his dream, though he knew he had little chance of success.

The streets of the city were **bedlam** during the earthquake. The noise and confusion were beyond anything anyone had seen before.

The writer always recalled her college **mentor**. She said that the professor's advice had always inspired her.

A **titanic** invasion of leaf cutter ants swept over the land. It was a gigantic infestation.

The movie contained a very **erotic** love scene. Its sexual nature earned it an R rating.

Number of words you recognize by sight, sound, or context: _____

Return to the list above and write down your own definition for each word based on the context clues from these sentences.

DEFINITIONS AND SOURCES

The words from today's list are defined below. There's also an explanation of the name that the word comes from, which will help you remember the meaning of the word.

bedlam: a scene of madness and confusion
Bethlehem hospital in London was an asylum for the insane.
chauvinistic: blindly loyal to a cause, gender, or country
The loyalty of Nicholas **Chauvin** to his leader, Napoleon, was legendary.
cynical: distrustful of the motives of others
The **Cynics** were a school of philosophy in ancient Greece who emphasized principles of self-reliance and criticism of society.
draconian: harsh and severe, usually pertaining to laws

The ancient Athenian lawmaker **Draco** is remembered for writing an extremely harsh code of laws.

erotic: pertaining to physical love

Eros was the god of love in Greek mythology.

forensic: pertaining to public speaking or to the legal aspects of medicine

The **forum** in ancient Rome was the place for public speaking and the center of the law courts.

gerrymander: to redraw district boundaries to favor a particular candidate

Elbridge **Gerry** was an 18th-century Massachusetts politician who redrew election lines to favor particular voting blocs. One such district resembled the outline of a salamander. Gerry's name was joined to the last part of *salamander* to make *gerrymander.*

jovial: happy, outgoing, sociable

In Greek mythology, **Jove** was the chief god. He smiled indulgently on his people.

masochist: one who takes pleasure in pain, particularly self-inflicted pain (The adjective form is **masochistic.**)

Leopold von Sacher **Masoch** was a 19th-century writer who found pleasure in being punished or abused.

maudlin: tearfully sentimental

In medieval art and theater, Mary **Magdalene** was often depicted as weeping excessively. The word *maudlin* comes from the old pronunciation of her name and indicates any weak emotionalism.

maverick: a political independent or nonconformist free spirit

Samuel **Maverick** was a Texas rancher who refused to brand his animals. Therefore, a person who doesn't follow institutional policy is considered to be a **maverick.**

mecca: a goal or place of pilgrimage for groups of people

Mecca, the birthplace of Mohammed in Arabia, is the goal of pilgrimages for the faithful of Islam.

mentor: a trusted advisor or counselor

In Greek mythology, **Mentor** was Odysseus's friend who guided his actions.

mesmerize: to fascinate, hold spellbound

Friedrich **Mesmer** was a 19th-century hypnotist, popular in Vienna and Paris for his theory of "animal magnetism."

narcissistic: self-absorbed, conceited

In Greek mythology, **Narcissus** was a handsome youth who drowned by falling into a pool in which he saw his own reflection.

quixotic: showing an impractical level of idealism

Miguel Cervantes's book *Don Quixote* is named for its hero, who pursues dreams that are really illusions, such as trying to joust with windmills because he thinks they are actually giants.

stoic: bearing suffering without complaint

The **Stoa** was an area in ancient Athens where a school founded by the philosopher Zeno met. The school emphasized emotional control and enduring hardships bravely.

tantalize: to tease or to hold just out of reach

Tantalus in Greek mythology was doomed to the underworld where everything he needed was in sight but out of reach.

titanic: gigantic (the noun form is **titan,** a giant)

The **Titans** were the gods of great strength and power in Greek mythology.

utopia: an ideal society

Thomas More's book *Utopia,* written in the sixteenth century, described an ideal state. The word is also used satirically as the name of the country in the twentieth-century novel *Brave New World* by Aldous Huxley.

PRACTICE

Complete Exercises 1 and 2 below, and then check your answers at the end of the lesson. If you score below 80 percent on either exercise, do Exercise 3 for additional practice.

Exercise 1

Match the words in the first column with their meanings in the second column.

_____ 1. jovial

_____ 2. draconian

_____ 3. quixotic

_____ 4. mentor

_____ 5. mesmerize

_____ 6. chauvinistic

_____ 7. stoic

_____ 8. titan

_____ 9. utopia

_____ 10. mecca

a. an ideal society

b. a wise counselor or friend

c. blindly loyal to a cause or a person

d. indifferent to pleasure or pain

e. a place of pilgrimage

f. a giant punished by the gods

g. foolishly idealistic

h. harsh, punitive

i. to hypnotize

j. jolly, sociable

k. a giant of great strength

Score on Exercise 1: _____

Exercise 2

Mark the following statements as true or false according to the meaning of the underlined words.

_____ 11. A cynical person would be suspicious of the motives of others.

_____ 12. Erotic love is physical attraction.

_____ 13. The purpose of gerrymandering a district is to ensure a balanced ticket.

_____ 14. Forensic skills are needed by trial lawyers.

_____ 15. A maverick is a party loyalist.

_____ 16. A narcissistic person would likely be a good gardener.

_____ 17. Bedlam would be a good place to seek peace and quiet.

_____ 18. Cooking smells would be tantalizing to a hungry man.

_____ 19. A maudlin person is asking for sympathy but isn't likely to get it.

_____ 20. A masochist always pursues pleasure and avoids pain.

Score on Exercise 2: _____

Exercise 3

Write in the blank the word from today's list that best fits the context clues given.

21. A _____, a society with an ideal way of life, is a dream, not a reality.

22. Though he professed to be interested in others, he was really _____ at heart.

23. He was a medical _____. He refused to follow the dictates of the hospital when treating critically ill patients.

24. Though she personally was quite upbeat and optimistic, her writing was full of _____ sentiments of death and loss.

25. Being the understudy in the show _____ her with a glimpse of stardom.

26. "Why do you stay in these abusive relationships?" he said. "You must be a real _____."

27. The football coach was a real _____ to the young men on his team. He spent a great deal of time offering them guidance and wise counsel.

28. In some countries torture and other _____ punishments await those who traffic in drugs.

29. Bill Gates is often considered a _____ in the computer industry. His company's giant presence dwarfs the competition.

30. He had become _____ in his old age. He distrusted the motives of most people with whom he came in contact.

Score on Exercise 3: _____

WRAP UP

Choose five words from Word List 8 and write each in a sentence below. In writing your sentences, try to give context clues, and identify the kind of context clue you have used. Write the remaining five words and their definitions on index cards to add to your Keeper List.

_____

_____

_____

_____

_____

ANSWERS

Exercise 1	Exercise 2	Exercise 3
1. j	11. true	21. utopia
2. h	12. true	22. narcissistic
3. g	13. false	23. maverick
4. b	14. true	24. maudlin
5. i	15. false	25. tantalized
6. c	16. false	26. masochist
7. d	17. false	27. mentor
8. k	18. true	28. draconian
9. a	19. true	29. titan
10. e	20. false	30. cynical

WORDS FROM THE WORLD OF WORK

LESSON SUMMARY

This lesson and the next focus on strategies for learning new words that will help you in your work. Today's word list includes terms that are used in all kinds of workplaces.

Like many adult learners, you probably want to use what you learn to maximize your earning power and your satisfaction with the work you do. As workers are displaced from their jobs, they have to become more flexible and have a broader awareness of the job market beyond the narrow area for which they first prepared. This lesson and the next present vocabulary of the workplace. This lesson focuses on general terms associated with employment, while Lesson 10 presents terms from new and emerging technologies that all workers must learn in order to keep up with trends in the workplace.

WORKING WITH WORD LIST 9

BY SIGHT AND SOUND

See how many of the following terms from the world of work you know by sight and sound.

arbitrage	*AR-bit-traj*
arbitration	*ar-bi-TRAY-shun*
beneficiary	*ben-uh-FISH-ee-er-ee*
capital	*KAP-i-tul*
consortium	*kun-SOR-shee-um*
deduction	*de-DUCK-shun*
discrimination	*dis-krim-uh-NAY-shun*
entitlement	*en-TIE-tul-ment*
entrepreneur	*en-truh-pruh-NOOR*
equity	*EK-wi-tee*
exempt	*eg-ZEMPT*
fiscal	*FIS-cul*
franchise	*FRAN-chize*
harassment	*huh-RASS-ment*
jargon	*JAR-gun*
nepotism	*NEP-uh-tiz-em*
perquisite	*PER-kwi-zit*
prospectus	*pruh-SPEK-tus*
subsidy	*SUB-si-dee*
tenure	*TEN-yoor*

Number of words you know by sight or sound: _____

BY CONTEXT

Now meet the words in context.

To look at the workplaces of many Americans today is to see a number of serious problems. Private industry has been marked by **fiscal** mismanagement that has threatened the financial well being of many large companies. Government **subsidies**, moneys that support smaller enterprises, have been vastly curtailed. Many workers still face **discrimination** in workplaces that choose not to hire or promote on the basis of sex, skin color, or ethnic background. Many public employment arenas have been accused of **nepotism**, in which workers related to persons in authority are given preference in hiring. The high cost of expensive **perquisites** ("perks") has led to many industries eliminating the special privileges accorded their executives. Men and women alike have faced sexual **harassment** at their jobs. This kind of intimidation has been threatening to workers who feel that they must give into the demands of their employers or lose their jobs. Even **tenured** faculty at colleges and universities are losing the security promised by their guarantee of permanent employment. The response to these problems has been in part a trend toward starting new businesses. This has created a whole new group of **entrepreneurs** who seek to organize and promote new ventures and often provide the **capital,** or start-up money, for that purpose.

Here are the rest of the words in context clue sentences. Next to each sentence, identify the kind of clue used: restatement (R), contrast (C), example (E), or definition (D).

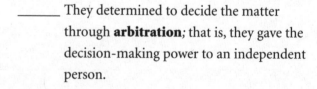

_____ He is the sole **beneficiary** of her estate. He will be given all the property when the old woman dies.

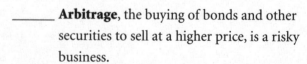

_____ They determined to decide the matter through **arbitration**; that is, they gave the decision-making power to an independent person.

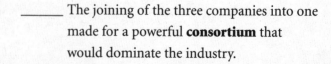

_____ **Arbitrage**, the buying of bonds and other securities to sell at a higher price, is a risky business.

_____ The joining of the three companies into one made for a powerful **consortium** that would dominate the industry.

_____ Restaurants like McDonald's and Burger King are **franchises** because they are allowed to operate under rules set out by the parent company.

_____ He took his children as tax **deductions** so that he could subtract the cost of their care from his taxes.

_____ The company published a **prospectus** to offer details of its plan for expansion. This plan offers potential investors pertinent information about the plan and the company.

_____ Though she was accused of being unfair in her demands, she claimed she only wanted **equity** in what was owed her.

_____ She was **exempt** from duty that day. She was excused because she had been injured.

_____ She felt that transportation money was an **entitlement**; that is, something that is hers by right.

_____ Learning the **jargon**, or language, of a particular interest or job is an important part of learning about the workplace.

Number of words you know by sight, sound, or context: _____

On a separate sheet of paper, write your own definitions for each word on List 9.

DEFINITIONS

Check the definitions you wrote against the definitions below. Did you come close?

arbitrage: the buying of "paper"—stocks, bonds, and securities—to resell for a quick profit

arbitration: the process by which disputes are settled by a third party

beneficiary: one who will benefit from something

capital: accumulated wealth, used to gain more wealth

consortium: a joining of two or more businesses for the purpose of dominating an industry

deduction: the subtraction of a cost from income

discrimination: the act of making distinctions in treatment between one group of people and another

entitlement: special privileges or benefits allowed to groups of people

entrepreneur: a businessperson whose special interest is in starting new companies

equity: fairness or evenness of treatment, or the value of property after all claims have been made against it

exempt: excused from some rule or job

fiscal: pertaining to money or finance

franchise: a business that is owned by a parent company but run by independent operators under rules set by the parent company

harassment: coercion or undue pressure

jargon: the specialized vocabulary of an industry or interest group

nepotism: the employment or promotion of friends and family members

prospectus: a published report of a business and its plans for a program or offering

subsidy: a grant of money for a particular purpose

tenure: the state or period of holding a particular position, or a guarantee of employment to teachers who have met particular standards

PRACTICE

Fill in the answers to Exercises 1 and 2 below. Check your answers at the end of the lesson. If you score below 80 percent on either exercise, do Exercise 3 for practice. Either way, do Test Practice questions.

Exercise 1

Match the words in the first column with their meanings in the second column.

_____ **1.** tenure

_____ **2.** jargon

_____ **3.** harassment

_____ **4.** deduction

_____ **5.** exempt

_____ **6.** perquisite

_____ **7.** subsidy

_____ **8.** franchise

_____ **9.** equity

_____**10.** entitlement

a. excused from

b. special privileges

c. financial support

d. a subtraction from the total

e. undue pressure

f. an addition to the total

g. benefits given to a particular group

i. state or term of employment

h. fairness

j. the language of a trade or job

k. a business owned by a parent company

Score on Exercise 1: _____

Exercise 2

Mark the following statements as true or false according to the meaning of the underlined words.

_____ **11.** Discrimination allows for fair hiring of all applicants.

_____ **12.** A consortium allows businesses to join together in the marketplace.

_____ **13.** The purpose of a prospectus is to explain the past history of a company.

_____ **14.** A beneficiary would gain nothing on the death of a policy holder.

_____ **15.** An entrepreneur is an independent businessman.

_____ **16.** Relatives of an executive whose company has rules against nepotism would be likely to get a job.

_____ **17.** Arbitrage involves the buying of securities for resale.

_____ **18.** In arbitration, disputes are settled by a disinterested third party.

_____ **19.** Most businesses need capital to get started.

_____ **20.** Fiscal transactions are financial in nature.

Score on Exercise 2: _____

Exercise 3

Fill in each blank with a word from Word List 9.

21. When you learn the language of a particular workplace, you are learning its _____.

22. If you use an independent person to settle a dispute, you are using _____.

23. If you manage a store according to the rules of a parent company, you own a _____.

24. We would all like to be _____ from paying too many taxes.

25. Promotions often bring _____, or special privileges.

26. When a teacher is given a guarantee of permanent employment, she has _____.

27. When you want to subtract certain expenses from your taxes, you want _____.

28. If you want information about a new offering by a company, you should read the _____.

29. If a boss subjects an employee to inappropriate pressure, the boss is guilty of _____.

30. The person who stands to gain from a bequest in a will is the _____.

Test Practice

Circle the correct word to complete each of the following sentences.

31. A teacher hopes to get (tenure/capital) to insure his or her employment.

32. Many labor disputes are settled by (arbitrage/arbitration).

33. Hiring or promoting relatives in a business is called (entitlement/nepotism).

34. A group of companies might join together to create a (franchise/consortium).

35. Special privileges enjoyed by a few employees are called (beneficiaries/perquisites).

36. When an employer takes unfair advantage of an employee it is called (harassment/discrimination).

37. When you seek to subtract an amount from the total you are seeking (equity/a deduction).

38. When you seek financial support you are looking for a(n) (exemption/subsidy).

39. For information about making an investment you should get advice from a(n) (prospectus/entrepreneur).

40. The language of the workplace is called (fiscal/jargon).

Test Tip

When you have to choose the word that fits in a given sentence from among two or more choices, restate the sentence as a true or false question using each choice. For example, in Test Practice question 38, restate the sentence using both choices:

When you seek financial support you are looking for a subsidy. True or false?

When you seek financial support you are looking for an exemption. True or false?

See which one makes the most sense. Also, look for a key word in the sentence that will give you a clue to the correct choice. In this question the word is *support.*

WRAP UP

Choose ten words from Word List 9. Write five of them in sentences on the blank lines, giving context clues whenever possible. Write the remaining five words and their definitions on index cards and add them to your Keeper List. Consider writing a sentence with a context clue on the cards to help you remember the words.

ANSWERS

Exercise 1	**Exercise 2**	**Exercise 3**	**Test Practice**
1. i	11. false	21. jargon	31. tenure
2. j	12. true	22. arbitration	32. arbitration
3. e	13. false	23. franchise	33. nepotism
4. d	14. false	24. exempt	34. consortium
5. a	15. true	25. perquisites	35. perquisites
6. b	16. false	26. tenure	36. harassment
7. c	17. true	27. deductions	37. a deduction
8. k	18. true	28. prospectus	38. subsidy
9. h	19. true	29. harassment	39. prospectus
10. g	20. true	30. beneficiary	40. jargon

L·E·S·S·O·N
WHAT'S THE GOOD (NEW) WORD?

10

LESSON SUMMARY
This lesson continues the study of how to learn new words by presenting new words from computer and communications technology.

Workplaces shift and expand around us, and our language also expands and changes. New words come into the language all the time. Many new words, for instance, have been created for the new technologies that drive so much of what people do. This lesson will help you learn some of the new terminology that surrounds us in the workplace and in the world.

WORKING WITH WORD LIST 10

BY SIGHT AND SOUND

See how many of these terms you recognize from seeing them written or from saying their pronunciation.

cursor	KUR-ser
cybernetics	sy-ber-NET-iks
database	DAY-ta-base
e-mail	EE-mail
hacker	HAK-er
hardware	HARD-wear
icon	EYE-kon
interface	IN-ter-face
Internet	IN-ter-net
modem	MO-dem
monitor	MON-it-er
mouse	MOWS
network	NET-werk
on-line	ON-line
peripherals	puh-RIF-ur-elz
software	SOFT-ware
spreadsheet	SPRED-sheet
user-friendly	YOO-zer FREND-ly
voice mail	VOYS mail
web sites	WEB sites

Number of words you know by sight and sound: _____

BY CONTEXT

Now see how many words you can add to your "known" list when you meet them in context.

To visit a computer supermarket these days is to step into a dizzying world of **cybernetics** by way of computer applications unimagined even a generation ago. A dazzling array of **software** packages allows a huge choice of programs to load onto the home computer. Brightly colored screens on **mon-itors,** or video display terminals, invite the browser to use a **mouse,** a **peripheral** that allows users to point to the operations they want to use on the computer. They can also explore the **Internet,** an international network of computer networks, connected by means of a telephone device called a **modem.** Interested consumers can learn how to correspond electronically from their home computers by **e-mail** and how to organize household accounts on a **spreadsheet** program that aids recordkeeping. It's part of the brave new world of computers—and the wave of the future for us all.

The industry had created a major **database** that held the information committed to its computer system.

He bought all the **hardware** he needed for his system, including a new hard drive.

He wanted his computer to **interface**, or connect and operate, with another system.

Her eyes followed the small blinking line, or **cursor**, that showed where the work was being done on the computer screen.

The system had been invaded by a **hacker**, someone who uses a computer to penetrate other computer systems and networks.

The new operating system offered an interesting array of **icons**, or small pictures on the screen that represent applications or files on the computer.

He left a message on her **voice mail,** the only way of reaching her when she was away.

The sales representative assured him that the system was **user-friendly,** that is, easy to operate and understand.

The writer was able to use the entire **network** of computers that shared a database.

He was thrilled to be able to locate information on a **web site**, a "location" on the Internet's World Wide Web.

The teacher wanted her students to be **on-line** at their computers so that they could have direct access to the information available on the Internet.

Number of words you recognize by sight, sound, or context: _____

DEFINITIONS

Below are the definitions for words from today's list. Use these definitions to help you complete the exercises that follow.

cursor: the small blinking light or line that signals where your data will be entered on a computer monitor

cybernetics: the study of computer technology

database: information stored in a specific format, usually available to a user through a computer

e-mail: electronic mail, written communication sent from one computer to another

hacker: a person who uses computers recreationally and sometimes illegally for the purpose of invading other computer systems and networks

hardware: the physical components of a computer system, including screen, keyboard, central processing unit, and so on

icon: a small picture that identifies an application or file on a computer

interface: the way in which two systems come together to perform a joint function

Internet: a group of networks accessible to the user via modems; vast quantities of information are available through the Internet

modem: a modulator/demodulator, a device that allows signals from one computer to speak to another computer through telephone lines

monitor: a video screen on which computer programs can be viewed

mouse: a pointing device that allows users to indicate on the screen what operation they want to use

network: a group of computers linked through a shared communication code

on-line: having direct access to information through the computer, usually by being connected to a computer network

peripherals: devices connected to computers which allow additional functions: printers, pointing devices such as a mouse or touchpad, and modems.

software: the programs that tell the computer what functions to perform

spreadsheet: a computer program that allows the user to enter and manipulate data, especially numbers

user-friendly: describes computer applications that are easy to learn and use

voice mail: a system that allows a telephone to take or leave messages electronically

web site: a "location" on the part of the Internet known as the World Wide Web, which provides graphics and sound as well as text

PRACTICE

Do Exercises 1 and 2 below. Check your answers at the end of the lesson. If you score below 80 percent on either one, do Exercise 3 for more practice.

Exercise 1

Match the word in the first column with its meaning in the second column.

_____ **1.** monitor

_____ **2.** cursor

_____ **3.** mouse

_____ **4.** modem

_____ **5.** icon

_____ **6.** software

_____ **7.** spreadsheet

_____ **8.** voice mail

_____ **9.** cybernetics

_____ **10.** e-mail

a. electronic message device

b. software for using figures

c. programs that tell the computer what to do

d. electronic written communication

e. computer video screen

f. device that allows two computers to interact

g. pointing device

h. computer technology

i. design programs

j. picture that indicates a computer application

k. indicator of your place on the computer screen

Score on Exercise 1: _____

Exercise 2

Mark the following statements as true or false according to the meaning of the underlined word.

_____**11.** <u>User-friendly</u> computers are popular among new computer users.

_____**12.** A <u>hacker</u> is a nickname for a professional computer engineer.

_____**13.** <u>Peripherals</u> can be used separately from the computer itself.

_____**14.** Computers communicate with each other through the <u>Internet</u>.

_____**15.** A computer <u>database</u> is a means of sorting and storing information.

_____**16.** A printer requires an <u>interface</u> with the computer.

_____**17.** A computer does not have to be <u>on-line</u> to get or give information.

_____**18.** <u>Hardware</u> refers to the programs available to load on the computer.

_____**19.** <u>Web sites</u> are programs for engineers.

_____**20.** A company usually has a <u>network</u> of computers that share data.

Score on Exercise 2:_____

Exercise 3

Fill in the blanks with words or terms from Word List 10.

21. A device that allows a computer to transfer information to another computer over telephone lines is called a(n) _____.

22. A pointing device that lets the user identify a particular application on a computer is a(n) _____.

23. Small pictures that indicate computer functions are _____.

24. You can use _____ to leave a message for someone electronically on the telephone.

25. A computer lover who uses computers to gain information, sometimes illegally, from many databases is called a _____.

26. The science of using computer technology to accomplish a communication or information goal is called _____.

27. The small signal that locates where computer activity is taking place is the _____.

28. A program that lets the user enter and calculate figures is called a _____.

29. Devices that are connected to a computer and perform related functions are called _____.

30. A group of networks that is accessible to users through the modem is called the _____.

Score on Exercise 3: _____

WRAP UP

Choose ten words or terms from Word List 10. Write five of them in sentences below.

_____

_____

_____

_____

_____

Write the other five words you've chosen and their definitions on index cards and add them to your Keeper List. You should have at least 50 words on your Keeper List by now. Ask a friend to quiz you on them.

ANSWERS

Exercise 1	Exercise 2	Exercise 3
1. e	11. true	21. modem
2. k	12. false	22. mouse
3. g	13. false	23. icons
4. f	14. true	24. voice mail
5. j	15. true	25. hacker
6. c	16. true	26. cybernetics
7. b	17. false	27. cursor
8. a	18. false	28. spreadsheet
9. h	19. false	29. peripherals
10. d	20. true	30. Internet

SPELLING

The beginning of this book showed you that you have to work to develop your vocabulary in part because other people judge you by the way you express yourself in speech and writing. The words you use are the most "public" reflection of your thoughts and feelings. Having a handsome vocabulary but letting the words appear poorly spelled, however, is like wearing a nice outfit but failing to comb your hair. The whole package doesn't make a nice appearance. The next set of lessons, then, is designed to help you make sure that the words you write for public consumption will look as good as they sound.

L·E·S·S·O·N

USING YOUR SENSES TO MAKE SENSE OUT OF SPELLING

LESSON SUMMARY

This lesson gives you some overall strategies for improving your spelling by showing you how to combine input from several different senses. You'll also learn the rules and exceptions for using *ie* and *ei* vowel combinations.

ou saw in the vocabulary section of this book that the English language is often phonetically irregular. If you simply wrote words the way they sound, you'd come up with some very peculiar spellings:

In the furst haf uv this buk wee lerned sum wayz to lurn noo wurds and to make them part uv our reeding, lisning, or speeking vokabyoolarryz.

The *eye* is often offended by spelling that *sounds* right, because it just looks too odd. Similarly, if you tried to sound out every word and pronounce it exactly the way it's written, you'd come up with some pretty odd pronunciations:

*In the second half of the book we will see how words (**wore**-dz?) require us to learn special (**spes**-ee-al?) techniques (techni-**cues**?) to help us see to it that we learn (l-**ear**-n?) to spell them accurately (aku-**rate**-ly?).*

The *ear* is offended by pronouncing what you see strictly according to the rules of phonics. That's why you have to use several different senses to learn to spell more accurately.

HOW TO LEARN TO SPELL

Here are some general multisensory tips for studying spelling:

- **Use your eyes.**
  Look at words carefully. With a marker or pen, highlight the part of the word that is hard to remember.
  Visualize the word with your eyes closed.
- **Use your ears.**
  Listen for the sound of words you hear in conversation or on the radio or television.
  Listen to the sound of the spelling of words: Ask someone to dictate the words and their spelling and listen as the word is spelled out.
- **Use your hands.**
  Write the word several times, spelling it in your head as you write.

There are two main stumbling blocks to spelling by sight and sound. One we have already identified—the fact that English is both phonetically inconsistent and visually confusing. Added to that is the problem of regional speech. In different parts of the United States, people pronounce words differently, often in ways that make it difficult to *hear* the proper spelling. For example:

- In some parts of the country, the word *asked* is pronounced *ast*. In other parts of the country, particularly the Northeast, you hear it pronounced *aksed*.
- In the South and some other areas, many people don't pronounce the final *g* in the *-ing* ending, so that you hear *goin, startin, restin*, and so on.
- In northern cities, some people pronounce *th* as *d*, so you hear *dese, dose*, and *dem.*

It's difficult, then, to put much faith in learning to spell words by sound alone. So here are four strategies that can guide your way through a difficult system and give you some ways to make good spelling a part of your life.

1. **Learn the rules, but expect some exceptions.** The lessons that follow point out both rules and exceptions for particular spelling difficulties.

2. **Use mnemonics (memory tricks) to help you remember how to spell unfamiliar or confusing words.** This book will give you some helpful memory hints, but you can come up with your own as well. For example, if you learn best by listening, make auditory cues from the sounds of words. If you learn best by sight, use visual cues such as coloring or highlighting key parts of the word.

3. **Use it or lose it.** Try to use each spelling word you learn in some meaningful way. As you write, say the spelling of the word in your head. When you use a word in conversation, try to remember what it looks like.

4. **Hang in there.** If you didn't do well in spelling in school, that doesn't mean you have to define yourself as a bad speller. As an adult learning to spell, you have a lot of advantages. Not the least of these is that you don't have to take those spelling tests every Friday!

Today's lesson deals with one of the old familiar spelling problems: words that contain *ie* or *ei* combinations.

WORDS THAT USE *IE*

The Rule

When the *ie* combination sounds like long *e* (*ee*), the rule is the one you learned in school:

i **before** *e* **except after** *c*.

Here are some examples of words that use *ie* to make the *ee* sound:

achieve	fiend	piece
belief	fierce	retrieve
bier	frieze	relieve
cashier	hygiene	siege
chief	niece	wield

The Exceptions

This isn't an exception but a new rule: When the combination sounds like *ay*, it is spelled *ei*. See the next section, where there is also a list of other words that use *ei*.

■ The *ie* combination can have other sounds besides *ee*:
    It can sound like short *e*, as in *friend*.
    It can sound like long *i*, as in *piety, fiery, quiet, notoriety, society, science*.
■ The *ie* combination comes after *c* when it sounds like *sh*, as in *ancient, deficient, conscience*.

Fortunately, there are no other exceptions to the **except after** *c* part of the rule. If there is a *c* with an *ei* after it, there's another letter in between, as in *achieve*. And you will see an *i* alone after a soft *c*, as in *circle* or *circumference*. But you will never see *c* followed directly by *ie* unless it sounds like *sh*.

Memory Tricks

Use the following tricks to help you remember some of the words.

■ There are enough *ie* words that you can make rhyming pairs: *grief/belief, reprieve/relieve*, and so on.
■ You can remember that the word *nice* is embedded in the word *niece*. Think, "I have a **nice** little **niece**."
■ You can remember that *piece* has the word *pie* in it. Think of a **pie**ce of **pie**.

In Context

You can use the words in context to help you remember their spellings. Fill in the missing letters in the following sentences:

1. It was his bel__ __f that all people are created equal.

2. He saw a beautiful painted fr__ __ze decorating the Greek temple.

3. The cash __ __r took the money at the rear of the store.

4. He was afraid that she might w__ __ld the weapon in a threatening manner.

5. The body of the king rested on a b__ __r in the great hall.

WORDS THAT USE *EI*

The Rules

You may have learned the basic *ei* rule as part of the *ie* rule above:

e comes before *i* when it sounds like *ay* as in *neighbor* and *weigh*.

Here are some examples of words in which *ei* makes the long *a* sound:

deign	heinous	surveillance
eight	inveigh	veil
feign	reign	vein
feint	skein	weight
freight	sleigh	

As you learned in the *ie* rule above, after *c* you use *ei*, even if it sounds like *ee*: *ceiling, deceit, conceited, receive, receipt.*

The Exceptions

You simply have to memorize some words that use the *ei* combination rather than *ie.*

- In some words, *ei* is used even though it sounds like *ee*: *either, seize, weird, sheik, seizure, leisure.*
- Sometimes *ei* sounds like long *i*: *height, sleight, stein, seismology.*
- Sometimes *ei* sounds like short *e*: *heifer, their, foreign, forfeit.*

Memory Tricks

Here are some memory tricks you can try to help you remember *ei* words:

- Try grouping several words in a sentence you'll remember because the words are related in meaning, for example, "The *conceited* girl tried to

deceive her parents by preventing them from *receiving* her school report."

- Highlight the *ei* combinations with a highlighter or pen. This will give you a visual cue.

In Context

Use the words in context to help you remember their spellings. (This will also help you learn the meanings of any words that are unfamiliar to you.) Fill in the correct letters in the words below:

1. The officer and his partner kept close surv__ __llance on the abandoned house.

2. He had to f__ __gn ignorance of her dishonesty.

3. It was a h__ __nous crime that was on the front pages for weeks.

4. The candidate began to inv___ __gh against what she said were abuses of power in the legislature.

5. The movie star d__ __ned to sign an autograph for her adoring fans.

PRACTICE

Now practice spelling words with *ie* and *ei* combinations. Complete Exercises 1 and 2 below, and check your answers at the end of the lesson. If you miss more than two words in either exercise, do Exercise 3 for additional practice. Otherwise, go directly to Test Practice.

Exercise 1

Fill in the blanks below with *ei* or *ie* to spell the word correctly.

1. The bride wore a v__ __l that had been in her family for generations.

2. The horse-drawn sl__ __gh sped across the icy landscape.

3. He taught the dog to retr__ __ve the ball when he threw it across the lawn.

4. She bought a sk__ __n of yarn to knit a new pair of socks for her husband.

5. The cash __ __r gave him a rec__ __pt for his purchase.

6. He added a new fr__ __ght car to his model train layout.

7. In hyg__ __ne class the students learned about good health.

8. He fought a f__ __rce battle over parking tickets.

9. He needed __ __ght dollars to pay for his dry cleaning.

10. He received an award for his lifetime of ach__ __vement.

Score on Exercise 1: _____

Exercise 2

Choose a word from today's lesson to complete each sentence below.

11. The archeologists found _____ documents in the tomb.

12. In his _____ time the author likes to play tennis.

13. His _____ bothered him when he told a lie to his wife.

14. He enjoyed the peace and _____ of a Sunday afternoon.

15. He didn't enjoy the endless parties that seemed to be expected of those in high _____.

16. The farmer took his prize _____ to the market for sale.

17. He looked on her not only as his doctor but also as his _____.

18. He said he wanted to go _____ to the movies or to a play.

19. Michael Jackson gained considerable _____ in the public mind after some lawsuits were brought against him.

20. He tried to _____, or pretend, enthusiasm for the concert.

Score on Exercise 2: _____

Exercise 3

Mark *C* if the underlined word is correctly spelled and *I* if it is incorrect. If the spelling is incorrect, write the correct spelling on the line next to the sentence.

_____ **21.** He had a beer <u>stien</u> that had belonged to his grandfather. _____

_____ **22.** He thought his sister's wardrobe from the thrift shop was just another one of her <u>wierd</u> ideas. _____

_____ **23.** The <u>ceiling</u> had long cracks that had appeared overnight. _____

_____ **24.** He committed a <u>hienous</u> crime and deserved to be punished. _____

_____ **25.** He suffered a brain <u>seizure</u> and was taken to the hospital. _____

_____ **26.** The World <u>Sereis</u> is played every fall. _____

_____ **27.** He set out to <u>achieve</u> great wealth, and he succeeded. _____

_____ **28.** They found a <u>vein</u> of ore in the abandoned mine. _____

_____ **29.** The magician used <u>slieght</u> of hand tricks to amaze his audience. _____

_____ **30.** He <u>befriended</u> a lonely old man who had no family of his own. _____

Score on Exercise 3: _____

Test Practice

Circle the word in the parentheses which is spelled correctly.

31. She took her (niece/neice) to the zoo on Saturday.

32. The agents were allowed to (sieze/seize) the narcotics at the border.

33. The doctor checked the baby's (hieght/height) and (weight/wieght).

34. He was very (relieved/releived) when the ordeal was over.

35. The (riegn/reign) of the new Miss America began that night.

36. They gave the (cashier/casheir) the money for the bill.

37. They had the criminal under (surviellance/surveillance) for over six months.

38. The (frieze/freize) at the Parthenon in Greece is one of the most famous works of art known to man.

39. The (chief/cheif) of police was under investigation for corruption while in office.

40. She believed him to be the (fiend/feind) who had stolen the old woman's inheritance.

WRAP UP

Choose ten words from this lesson that are new to your vocabulary or that you find hard to remember how to spell. Write five of them five times each on the blank lines. Write the other five on your Keeper List. Check your spelling. If you misspell any word, write it on a card and refer to it several times a day until you remember the spelling.

_____

_____

_____

_____

_____

ANSWERS

Exercise 1	Exercise 2	Exercise 3	Test Practice
1. veil	11. ancient	21. I, stein	31. niece
2. sleigh	12. leisure	22. I, weird	32. seize
3. retrieve	13. conscience	23. C	33. height, weight
4. skein	14. quiet	24. I, heinous	34. relieved
5. cashier, receipt	15. society	25. C	35. reign
6. freight	16. heifer	26. I, Series	36. cashier
7. hygiene	17. friend	27. C	37. surveillance
8. fierce	18. either	28. C	38. frieze
9. eight	19. notoriety	29. I, sleight	39. chief
10. achievement	20. feign	30. C	40. fiend

L·E·S·S·O·N 12

MORE TRICKY VOWELS

LESSON SUMMARY

This lesson shows you strategies for spelling words with various vowel combinations. It also helps you learn how to spell words that have silent vowels, as well as how to spell homophones, words that sound alike but have different meanings and are spelled differently.

esson 11 started with the most common vowel combination that gets in the way of spelling: the *ie/ei* pair. This lesson works with more words with vowels and vowel combinations that are difficult to spell.

VOWEL COMBINATIONS

The Rule

You may remember the old rhyme from school days, "When two vowels go walking, the first one does the talking and says its own name." That leads to the phonetic rule:

When two vowels are together, the first one is usually long ("says its own name") and the second one is silent.

For example, in the word *reach*, you hear long *e*, but not the short *a*. Similarly, if you know how to pronounce the word *caffeine*, you stand a chance at spelling it correctly because you hear that the *e* sound comes first.

If you know what sound you hear, that sound is likely to be the first of two vowels working together. This is particularly true of the *ai*, *ui*, and *ea* combinations—but see the next section for some exceptions with *ai*.

Here are some examples of words using *ai*, *ui*, and *ea* combinations in which the vowel you hear is the one that comes first.

abstain	prevail	nuisance
acquaint	refrain	cheapen
chaise	traipse	conceal
paisley	juice	heal

The Exceptions

There are several exceptions to this rule, which you will simply have to recognize by sight rather than by sound.

porcelain
beauty
healthy
hearse
hearty

Memory Tricks

You can use memory tricks to help you learn the exceptions.

- Remember the word *heart* is in *hearty*. Think: "A **hearty** person is good *hearted*."
- Some people put *ice* in *juice*. Think: "*Juice* is cooler if you add *ice*."
- The word *heal* appears in *healthy*. Think: "The doctor will *heal* you and help you stay **healthy**."

In Context

You can use the words in context to help you learn them. Fill in the missing vowel combinations in these words:

1. We had to tr___ ___pse all over town to find the right shoes.

2. She lay on a ch___ ___se lounge on the terrace.

3. She was a great b___ ___uty in her youth.

4. She decided that she would abst___ ___n from voting since she had not been present for the discussion.

5. His tie had a p___ ___sley pattern that was very attractive.

WORDS WITH *AI* OR *IA*

The Rules

It can be difficult to figure out when to use *ai* and when to use *ia*. Here are the rules, which cover most words:

When the vowel pair has one sound and says "uh" (e. g., *captain*), it uses *ai*.
When the vowel pair has separate sounds (e. g., *genial*), it uses *ia*.

Here are some examples:

Britain	fountain	familiar
captain	villain	genial
certain	alleviate	guardian
chieftain	brilliant	median
curtain	civilian	menial

The Exception

- Some words combine *t* or *c* with *ia* to make a *shuh* sound: *martial, beneficial, glacial.*

LearningExpress

20 Academy Street, P.O. Box 7100, Norwalk, CT 06852-9879

To provide you with the best test prep, basic skills, and
career materials, we would appreciate your help.
Please answer the following questions and return this postage paid piece.
Thank you for your time!

Name : _____

Address : _____

_____

Age : _____   Sex : ☐ Male   ☐ Female

Highest Level of School Completed : ☐ High School ☐ College

1) I am currently :

   A student — Year/level: _____

   Employed — Job title: _____

   Other — Please explain: _____

2) Jobs/careers of interest to me are :

   1. _____

   2. _____

   3. _____

3) If you are a student, did your guidance/career counselor provide
you with job information/materials?_____

4) What newspapers and/or magazines do you subscribe to or
read regularly?_____
_____

5) Do you own a computer?_____

   If so, do you have Internet access? _____

   How often do you go on-line?_____

6) The last time you visited a bookstore, did you make a purchase?

_____

Have you purchased career-related materials from bookstores?

_____

7) Do you subscribe to cable TV? _____

   Which channels to you watch regularly (please give network
   letters rather than channel numbers)?

   _____

   _____

8) Which radio stations do you listen to regularly (please give call
   letters and city name)?

   _____

   _____

9) How did you hear about the book you just purchased from
   LearningExpress?

   An ad?_____

   If so, where?_____

   An order form in the back of another book?_____

   A recommendation? _____

   A bookstore?_____

   Other?_____

10) Title of the book this card came from:

   _____

LearningExpress books are also available in the test prep/study guide section of your local bookstore.

LearningExpress

The leading publisher of customized career and test preparation books!

LearningExpress is an affiliate of Random House, Inc.

Memory Tricks

You can use the following tricks to help fix the rules about *ai* and *ia* in your memory:

- Spell out *captain* or *refrain* in your head to remember the *ai* pair.
- Make index cards with the vowel combinations and example words in separate columns.

In Context

Fill in the blanks with *ai* or *ia* to help you remember these combinations.

1. She was promoted to the rank of capt __ __n.

2. He was a gen__ __l host and made everyone feel welcome.

3. He saw that the ring had an artific__ __l diamond in the center.

4. She thought she saw a famil__ __r face in the crowd.

5. He was cert__ __n that he had seen her somewhere.

WORDS WITH SILENT VOWELS

One of the problems with spelling by sound is that some vowels in a word may not be pronounced. It's easy to forget to include such vowels in the spelling. There is no rule to guide you in spelling these words, though you can use memory tricks and context to help you remember them. The following list includes many of the most common words that have lost their vowels in pronunciation. The silent vowels are highlighted for you.

accidentally	chocolate	miniature
average	every	parliament
beverage	jewels	privilege
boundary	marriage	sophomore
carriage	mathematics	

Memory Tricks

Since there are no rules governing words with silent vowels, you just have to memorize them. Use one or both of these hints, depending on what works best for you:

- If you learn best by hearing, pronounce the silent letter to yourself every time you write the words. Say, for example, *soph-o-more* and *ev-er-y*.
- If you are a visual learner, write the words on cards, but use a different color ink for the silent letter.

In Context

Here's your first shot at learning the words with silent vowels. Add the missing vowels in the words below.

When Joseph was a soph__more in high school, his grades in math__matics dropped badly and his entire av__rage suffered. When his report card came, he was so upset that he accident__lly dropped his choc__late bev__rage all over the family's min__ature poodle and lost his TV priv__leges for a week.

WORDS THAT SOUND ALIKE BUT ARE SPELLED DIFFERENTLY

A number of words are easily confused because they are *homophones,* words that sound alike but are spelled differently. Many of these words have just one change in the vowel or vowel combination. There's no rule about these words, but you can learn them using memory tricks and context practice.

Here are examples of troublesome word pairs:

affect/effect
altar/alter
bare/bear
coarse/course
dual/duel
led/lead
minor/miner
peal/peel
piece/peace
sheer/shear
stationery/stationary
weak/week

Memory Tricks

Sometimes it helps to learn each word in terms of the job it will do in a sentence. Often the two words in a homophone pair are a different part of speech.

■ He led a **dual** (*adjective*) life as a spy.
He fought a **duel** (*noun*) with his great enemy.
■ He had to **alter** (*verb*) his clothes after he lost weight.
The bride smiled as she walked toward the **altar** (*noun*).
■ His words had a great **effect** (*noun*) on me.
The test score will not **affect** (*verb*) your final grade.

In Context

Since the meaning of each word in a homophone pair is different, context can be a great help in learning their spellings. Circle the word that belongs in each sentence below. The answers are directly below the sentences.

1. He felt (week/weak) after losing so much blood.

2. I can't (bare/bear) to leave the house looking like this.

3. He couldn't drink alcohol because he was a (miner/minor).

4. He had to (peel/peal) five pounds of potatoes for dinner.

5. There were (shear/sheer) curtains hanging on the window.

(Answers: weak, bear, minor, peel, sheer)

PRACTICE

Now practice spelling today's words. Complete Exercises 1 and 2, and check your answers at the end of the lesson. If you score less than 80 percent on either exercise, do Exercise 3 for additional practice.

Exercise 1

Fill in the missing letters in the words below.

1. It became a n__ __sance to have to drive five miles to the nearest store.

2. He gave his fiancee many beautiful jew__ls during their courtship.

3. He didn't want to ch__ __pen the effect by adding extra decorations.

4. She was elected to parl__ __ment before she was 40 years old.

5. The elderly butler said it was a priv__lege to work for such a distinquished family.

6. He tried to conc__ __l the contents of the box.

7. No soph__more may be seen in the vicinity.

8. The porcel__ __n vase was of museum quality.

9. She grew min__ __ture roses for the flower show.

10. She accident__lly fell over the antique chair in the foyer.

Score on Exercise 1: _____

Exercise 2

Circle the correct spelling of the word in parentheses in each of the sentences below.

11. He ordered a cold (beverage/beverege) after dinner.

12. He studied (mathmatics/mathematics) in college.

13. A (hearse/hurse) went by carrying the body of the prime minister.

14. The metal sculpture had a certain rough (beuty/beauty).

15. He went into (peels/peals) of laughter at the old Laurel and Hardy movies.

16. She asked for the (bare/bear) facts, not a lot of opinions.

17. His back needed to (heal/heel) before he could return to work.

18. She took a (coarse/course) in first aid with the Red Cross.

19. He rode a (stationary/stationery) bike for exercise.

20. The (porcelen/porcelain) figurine was the old woman's prize possession.

Score on Exercise 2: _____

Exercise 3

Mark C if the spelling of the underlined word is correct and I if it is incorrect. If the word is incorrect, spell it on the line following the sentence.

_____**21.** He took a <u>coarse</u> in auto repair.
_____

_____**22.** He was allergic to <u>chocolate</u>.
_____

_____**23.** She said that the secret to a happy <u>marrage</u> is compromise. _____

_____**24.** He fought a <u>dual</u> for the love of the fair maiden. _____

_____**25.** His illness made it necessary to <u>abstain</u> from liquor. _____

_____**26.** She wore <u>shear</u> stockings with her new summer dress. _____

_____**27.** The <u>minor</u> worked long hours underground for low pay. _____

_____**28.** She had a <u>hearty</u> laugh that rang through the crowded room.
_____

_____**29.** She bought an automatic <u>jiucer</u> for her cousin's birthday. _____

_____**30.** She was a <u>mathmatics</u> major in college.

_____

Score on Exercise 3: _____

WRAP UP

Choose ten words that are new to your vocabulary or that you find difficult to spell. Write five of them in sentences below. Write the other five on index cards to add to your Keeper List.

_____

_____

_____

_____

_____

ANSWERS

Exercise 1
1. nuisance
2. jewels
3. cheapen
4. parliament
5. privilege
6. conceal
7. sophomore
8. porcelain
9. miniature
10. accidentally

Exercise 2
11. beverage
12. mathematics
13. hearse
14. beauty
15. peals
16. bare
17. heal
18. course
19. stationary
20. porcelain

Exercise 3
21. I, course
22. C
23. I, marriage
24. I, duel
25. C
26. I, sheer
27. I, miner
28. C
29. I, juicer
30. I, mathematics

CONFUSING CONSONANTS

LESSON SUMMARY

This lesson deals with spelling problems caused by consonants. It shows you how to spell words with silent consonants, when to double consonants, and how to deal with consonants that can sound like other consonants.

essons 11 and 12 dealt with vowels and vowel combinations that are easily misused and confused. This lesson turns to consonants that make words difficult to spell.

SILENT CONSONANTS

Many English words include silent consonants, ones that are written but not pronounced. Alas, there is no rule governing silent consonants; you simply have to learn the words by sight. On the following page are some common examples, with the silent consonants highlighted:

answer	gnaw	pseudonym
autumn	indict	psychology
blight	kneel	rhetorical
calm	knight	subtle
debt	knowledge	through
ghost	often	write
gnarled	psalm	

Memory Tricks

Use sound cues or sight cues, depending on which works better for you—or use both to reinforce your learning.

- Pronounce the silent consonents in your mind as you write them. Say **subtle, often,** and so on.
- Write the words on index cards and highlight the missing consonant sounds with a marker.

In Context

Here are some sentences to help you learn the words in context. With the help of the list above, fill in the missing letters in the words below.

1. The dog likes to __naw on the bone in the back yard.

2. He wanted to pay his de__t to society.

3. He looked as though he might have seen a g__ost.

4. He wanted to study __sychology in college.

5. She thought that autum__ was the loveliest time of the year.

WHEN TO DOUBLE CONSONANTS

Most of the time a final consonant is doubled when you add an ending. *Drop* becomes *dropping*, *mop* becomes *mopping*, *stab* becomes *stabbing*. But what about *look/looking*, *rest/resting*, *counsel/counseled*?

The Rules

There are two sets of rules: one for when you're adding an ending that begins with a vowel (such as *-ed, –ing, –ance, –ence, –ant*) and another set for when the ending begins with a consonant (such as *-ness* or *-ly*).

1. When the ending begins with a vowel:

    Double the last consonant in a one syllable word that ends with one vowel and one consonant. For example, *flip* becomes *flipper* or *flipping*, *quit* becomes *quitter* or *quitting*, and *clap* becomes *clapper* or *clapping*.

    Double the final consonant when the last syllable is accented and there is only one consonant in the accented syllable. For example, *acquit* becomes *acquitting*, *refer* becomes *referring*, and *commit* becomes *committing*.

2. When the ending begins with a consonant:

    Keep a final _n_ when you add _-ness_. You end up with a double _n_: *keenness, leanness*.

    Keep a final _l_ when you add _-ly_. You end up with a double _l_: *formally, regally, legally*.

In other cases, then, you don't double the consonant.

The Exceptions

There are exceptions to the above rules, but not many. Here are a few of them:

- *Bus* becomes *buses*.
- *Chagrin* becomes *chagrined*.
- *Draw* becomes *drawing*.

Memory Tricks

You can remember a shorter version of the rules about doubling before an ending that begins with a vowel: **one** syllable or accented **last** syllable doubles the single consonant.

In Context

With the help of the rules above, add *-ed, –ing, –ness,* or *–ly* to the words below. Double the consonant if necessary.

1. He was strum_____ on the guitar on the back porch.

2. He wanted to go camp_____ down by the lake.

3. She excel_____ at math and science.

4. He set the valuable vase down very careful____.

5. The model was known for her extraordinary thin_____.

TROUBLESOME CONSONANTS: *C* AND *G*

Two letters—*c* and *g*—offer special challenges for spelling by sight and sound.

The Rules

The letters *c* and *g* can sound either soft or hard. When *c* is soft, it sounds like *s;* when it's hard, it sounds like *k*. When *g* is soft, it sounds like *j;* when it's hard, it sounds like *g* as in *guess.* But the difference isn't as confusing at it seems at first.

The letters *c* and *g* are soft when followed by *e, i,* or *y*. Otherwise they are hard.

Thus, *c* sounds like *s* when it is followed by *e, i,* or *y,* as in *central, circle, cycle.* It sounds like *k* when followed by other vowels: *case, cousin, current.*

This also means that *g* sounds like *j* when followed by *e, i,* or *y,* as in *genius, giant, gym.* When followed by other vowels, *g* is hard: *gamble, go, gun.*

A correlary to the rule about soft and hard *c* is this one:

A *k* is added to a final *c* before an ending that begins with *e, i,* or *y.*

If you didn't add the *k,* the *c* would become soft and sound like *s.* So in order to add *-ing* to *panic,* for example, you have to put a *k* first: *panicking.*

Here are some examples of words in which *e, i,* or *y* makes a soft *c* or *g.*

Hear Ye, Hear Ye!

Be careful: Doubling a consonant may change the word into a different word and the different meaning.

- *Planning* is different from *planing.*
- *Scrapping* is different from *scraping.*
- *Pinning* is different from *pining.*

    After you have doubled a consonant, look at it and sound it out. Does it mean what you need it to mean?

---

centimeter	general
centrifuge	generous
circulate	genteel
circus	germ
cyclical	giraffe
cymbal	gyrate

Here are some examples of words that have had a *k* added to *c* before an ending beginning with *e*, *i*, or *y*.

mimicking	picnicked
panicky	trafficking

Memory Trick

There are virtually no exceptions to the rules about using *c* and *g*. Listen to the words as you spell them and let the rule guide your choice: *c*, *s*, or *k*; *g* or *j*.

In Context

Using the list above, add the missing letters to the words below:

1. The crashing of the c__mbal made them all pay attention.

2. He was a g__nerous man who gave willingly of what he had.

3. He was arrested for traffic__ing in drugs.

4. The g__neral ordered the troops into battle.

5. The fan helped to c__rculate the air.

HOMOPHONES AND OTHER SIMILAR WORDS

Some words sound the same but are spelled with small changes in consonants:

- **bloc** (noun meaning *group, coalition*)
  block (verb meaning *stop, hinder* or noun meaning *a square*)
- **cite** (verb meaning *quote or mention*)
  site (noun meaning *place*)
  sight (noun having to do with seeing)
- **cord** (noun meaning *thin rope*)
  chord (noun referring to a set of musical notes)
- **dessert** (noun meaning *what you eat after dinner*)
  desert (verb meaning *abandon*)
- **passed** (verb, the past tense of *pass*)
  past (noun or adjective referring to time before)
- **write** (verb having to do with putting words on paper)
  right (adjective meaning *correct*)

Other words sound almost the same but mean different things and contain different consonants:

- **advise** (verb, rhymes with *wise*)
  advice (noun, rhymes with *ice*)
- **devise** (verb, rhymes with *wise*)
  device (noun, rhymes with *ice*)
- **dissent** (noun meaning *disagreement*)
  descent (noun having to do with going down)
- **later** (adverb meaning *at a future time*)
  latter (adjective meaning *not the first*)

Once again, there are no rules to help you here, but you can learn the words using memory tricks and context.

Memory Tricks

You simply have to remember the homophones and near-homophones. Here are some ways to do so:

- Using a deck of index cards, write each word of several homophone pairs on a separate card. Mix them up and put them face down on a table. Ask someone to play Concentration with you and take turns matching the homonym pairs.

- Remember that homophones often have different parts of speech. Listening to or watching for how a word is used in a sentence can often signal which word is needed.

In Context

Since the homophones have different meanings, context can be a great help in choosing which word to use. Circle the correct homophone in the following sentences. The answers are right after the sentences.

1. Can you (advise/advice) me as to what to do?

2. We ate a delicious (desert/dessert) at her house last night.

3. He invented a clever (devise/device) that would help him reach goods on high shelves.

4. A year (passed/past) before we knew what had happened to our friends.

5. He wanted to go (latter/later), but we all voted to leave immediately.

(**Answers:** advise, dessert, device, passed, later)

PRACTICE

Now practice your spelling strategies. Complete Exercises 1, 2, and 3, and check your answers at the end of the lesson. If you score less than 80 percent on any exercise, complete Exercise 4. If you score 80 percent or better, go right on to Test Practice.

Exercise 1

This exercise has to do with silent consonants. Fill in the missing letters in the words below.

1. __night

2. ans__er

3. de__t

4. __narled

5. indi__t

6. __salm

7. su__tle

8. g__ost

9. of__en

10. autum__

Score on Exercise 1: _____

Exercise 2

This exercise focuses on double consonants. Choose an appropriate ending for each word: *-ed, –ing, –ness,* or *-ly*. Rewrite the word on the line that follows it, doubling the consonant if necessary.

11. final _____

12. submit _____

13. hope _____

14. roam _____

15. control _____

16. plain _____

17. rebel (v) _____

18. throb _____

19. legal _____

20. rain _____

Score on Exercise 2: _____

Exercise 3

This exercise is on homophones. Circle the correct form of the word for each phrase below.

21. a new building (cite/site)

22. a voting (bloc/block)

23. the (right/write) to bear arms

24. a telephone (cord/chord)

25. to refer to the (later/latter)

26. sometime in the (passed/past)

27. the airplane's (dissent/descent)

28. to (device/devise) a new method

29. a fattening (dessert/desert)

30. to give good (advise/advice)

Score on Exercise 3: _____

Exercise 4

Write *C* in the blank if the underlined word or words are spelled correctly and *I* if the word or words are spelled incorrectly. Write the correct spelling of any misspelled words in the blank(s) following the sentence.

_____ **31.** She was a genteel woman of great <u>refinement</u>. _____

_____ **32.** There was a <u>sutle</u> hint of <u>autum</u> in the air. _____ _____

_____ **33.** He was a dedicated soldier and did not want to <u>dessert</u> his post. _____

_____ **34.** The baby was <u>colicy</u> and kept his parents awake all night. _____

_____ **35.** He visited the building <u>cite</u> several times a week. _____

_____ **36.** He was <u>transferred</u> to another job last week. _____

_____ **37.** He was <u>acquitted</u> of the crime of murder. _____

_____ **38.** He was <u>planing</u> to go home after work. _____

_____ **39.** He <u>strumed</u> a <u>cord</u> on his guitar to get everyone's attention. _____ _____

_____ **40.** His <u>meanness</u> was legendary in the company. _____

Score on Exercise 4: _____

Test Practice

Circle the letter of the word that is correctly spelled in each group below.

41. a. curculate
   b. circulate
   c. cercullate
   d. circulat

42. a. traficking
   b. trafficing
   c. traficing
   d. trafficking

43. a. pseudonym
   b. pseudonim
   c. pseudonymn
   d. psuedonym

44. a. girate
   b. gyrate
   c. jirate
   d. jyrate

45. a. retorical
   b. rhetorikal
   c. rhetorical
   d. retorecle

46. a. anser
   b. answer
   c. answir
   d. ansur

47. a. drawwing
   b. drauing
   c. drawing
   d. draweng

48. a. lableing
b. labulling
c. labeling
d. labiling

49. a. genoside
b. genocied
c. jenocide
d. genocide

50. a. genaris
b. generus
c. genarous
d. generous

WRAP UP

Choose ten words from this lesson that are unfamiliar or difficult to spell. Write five of them five times each below. Write the other five on your Keeper List index cards.

_____

_____

_____

_____

_____

ANSWERS

Exercise 1

1. knight
2. answer
3. debt
4. gnarled
5. indict
6. psalm
7. subtle
8. ghost
9. often
10. autumn

Exercise 2

11. finally
12. submitting, submitted
13. hoping, hoped
14. roaming, roamed
15. controlling, controlled
16. plainness
17. rebelling, rebelled
18. throbbing, throbbed
19. legally
20. raining, rained

Exercise 3

21. site
22. bloc
23. right
24. cord
25. latter
26. past
27. descent
28. devise
29. dessert
30. advice

Exercise 4

31. C
32. I, subtle, autumn
33. I, desert
34. I, colicky
35. I, site
36. C
37. C
38. I, planning
39. I, strummed, chord
40. C

Test Practice

41. b
42. d
43. a
44. b
45. c
46. b
47. c
48. c
49. d
50. d

TRICKY ENDINGS

14

LESSON SUMMARY

This lesson shows you when to keep and when to drop a final *e* or final *y* when you add a suffix.

ord endings often present difficulties in spelling. It's hard to remember when to drop letters and when to keep them. This lesson will nail down some simple rules to help you with those decisions.

WHEN TO DROP A FINAL *E*

There are two rules covering whether to drop a final *e* when you add a suffix: one for when you drop it and one for when you keep it.

Rule 1

Drop the final *e* when you add an ending that begins with a vowel.

Here are some examples of words that use this rule.

- With *-ing*
  change + *-ing* = *changing*
  receive + *-ing* = *receiving*
  surprise + *-ing* = *surprising*

- With *-able*

  argue + -able = arguable

  desire + -able = desirable

  erase + -able = erasable

- With *-ous*

  grieve + -ous = grievous

  pore + -ous = porous

  virtue + -ous = virtuous

- With *-ity*

  intense + –ity = intensity

  opportune + -ity = opportunity

  scarce + –ity = scarcity

The Exceptions

- Keep the final *e* after soft *c* or soft *g* in order to keep the soft sound.

  peace + -able = peaceable

  advantgage + –ous = advantageous

  courage + –ous = courageous

  outrage + –ous = outrageous

- Keep the final *e* in other cases when you need to protect pronunciation.

  shoe + –ing = shoeing (not *shoing*)

  guarantee + –ing = guaranteeing (not *guaranteing*)

Memory Trick

The best way to remember these words is to sound them out after you spell them. If it doesn't *sound* right, the chances are the spelling is incorrect.

In Context

Use context to help you remember the rule above. Write the following combinations in the blanks provided, keeping or omitting the final *e* as necessary.

1. It was a (surprise + –ing) _____ ending.

2. The real estate agent said that the property would be very (desire + –able) _____ in the market.

3. The astronauts were remarkably (courage + –ous) _____ men and women.

4. The storm brought a (scarce + –ity) _____ of fresh food and electricity.

5. The Quakers are a (peace + –able) _____ people.

Rule 2

Keep the final *e* before endings that begin with consonants.

Here are some examples of words that use this rule.

- With *-ment*

  advertise + –ment = advertisement

  amuse + –ment = amusement

  enforce + –ment = enforcement

- With *-ness*

  appropriate + –ness = appropriateness

  fierce + –ness = fierceness

  polite + –ness = politeness

- With *–less*

  care + –less = careless

  sense + –less = senseless

  tire + –less = tireless

- With *-ful*

  disgrace + –ful = disgraceful

  grace + –ful = graceful

  shame + –ful = shameful

The Exception

There's one important exception to the rule about keeping the final *e* when you add an ending that begins with a consonant:

■ Drop the final *e* when it occurs after the letters *u* or *w*.

argue + *–ment* = *argument*
awe + *–ful* = *awful*
true + *–ly* = *truly*

In Context

Use context to help you remember the rule and its exception. Rewrite the words with the endings in the blanks below:

1. He read a great (advertise + –ment) _____ in the paper today.

2. He had to learn not to be so (care + –less) _____ with his wallet.

3. He was known for his (polite + –ness) _____ and good manners.

4. They had an (argue + –ment) _____ on the phone.

5. He left the room in a (disgrace + –ful) _____ condition.

WHEN TO KEEP A FINAL *Y* OR CHANGE IT TO *I*

Rule 1

When you add a suffix to a word ending in *y*, keep the *y* if it follows a vowel.

This time it doesn't matter whether the suffix begins with a vowel or a consonant. Always keep the *y*

if it comes immediately after a vowel. Here are some examples:

■ With *-s*
attorney + *–s* = *attorneys*
chimney + *–s* = *chimneys*
■ With *-ed*
delay + *–ed* = *delayed*
play + *–ed* = *played*
■ With *-ing*
cloy + *–ing* = *cloying*
relay + *–ing* = *relaying*
■ With *-ance*
annoy + *–ance* = *annoyance*
convey + *–ance* = *conveyance*
■ With *-able*
enjoy + *–able* = *enjoyable*
employ + *–able* = *employable*

The Exceptions

Some words break this rule and change the *y* to *i*.

Day becomes *daily*.
Pay becomes *paid*.
Say becomes *said*.

In Context

Use context to help you remember the rule. Rewrite the words with their suffixes in the blanks below.

1. We hired two (attorney + –s) _____ to handle the case.

2. She insisted on (relay + –ing) _____ the message to her father.

3. I found the movie very (enjoy + –able) _____.

4. The children were (play + –ing) _____ outdoors.

5. The mosquitos were a serious (annoy + –ance) _____.

Rule 2

When you add a suffix to a word ending in _y_, keep the _y_ if it follows a consonant.

Again, it doesn't matter whether the suffix begins with a vowel or a consonant. Here are some examples:

- With -_ful_
  beauty + –_ful_ = _beautiful_
  mercy + –_ful_ = _merciful_
  plenty + –_ful_ = _plentiful_
- With -_ness_
  busy + –_ness_ = _business_
  dizzy + –_ness_ = _dizziness_
  lonely + –_ness_ = _loneliness_
- With -_ly_
  angry + –_ly_ = _angrily_
  busy + –_ly_ = _busily_
  hearty + –_ly_ = _heartily_
- With -_es_
  comedy + –_es_ = _comedies_
  hurry + –_es_ = _hurries_
  salary + –_es_ = _salaries_

The Exception
There's one group of exceptions to the above rule.

- When you add -_ing_, keep the final _y_.
  bury + –_ing_ = _burying_
  copy + –_ing_ = _copying_
  study + –_ing_ = _studying_

In Context
Using the rule in context will help you remember it. Rewrite the words with their suffixes in the blanks below.

1. He always (hurry + –es) _____ to get to school early.

2. The lumberjack ate (hearty + –ly) _____ through a stack of pancakes.

3. She spent all her spare time (study + –ing) _____ for the exam.

4. He (angry + –ly) _____ slammed the door.

5. There was a (plenty + –ful) _____ supply of fish in the lake.

PRACTICE

Complete Exercises 1 and 2 below and check your answers at the end of the lesson. If you score less than 80 percent on either exercise, complete Exercise 3 for more practice.

Exercise 1
Choose the correctly spelled word in each of the following sentences.

1. He wore everyone out with his (intenseity/intensity).

2. She was tired of (receiving/receiveing) so much junk mail.

3. He wanted to make a career in law (enforcment/enforcement)

4. She was (busyly/busily) redecorating their new home.

5. They had both (chimneys/chimnies) cleaned.

6. She was anxious about (carrying/carring) the bad news to her mother.

7. We had a terrible (arguement/argument) over politics last night.

8. She was a (pityful/pitiful) sight when she came in drenched from the rain.

9. The house was in a (desirable/desireable) area.

10. He (truely/truly) loved his job and was anxious to succeed.

Score on Exercise 1: _____

Exercise 2

Mark *C* in the first blank if the underlined word is spelled correctly and *I* if it is spelled incorrectly. If the word is misspelled, write the correct spelling on the line following the sentence.

_____**11.** There are a number of good headache <u>remedys</u> on the market today.
_____

_____**12.** He had made a <u>grievious</u> error on his tax form. _____

_____**13.** He thought the job change would be <u>advantageous</u> to him. _____

_____**14.** She complained of <u>dizzyness</u> in the hot weather. _____

_____**15.** The starting <u>salaries</u> for college graduates are not always competitive.
_____

_____**16.** It was an <u>outrageous</u> mistake.
_____

_____**17.** He bore an <u>unmistakeable</u> resemblance to his father. _____

_____**18.** He had a number of opportunities to expand his <u>business</u>. _____

_____**19.** He read a number of good <u>mysterys</u> on his vacation. _____

_____**20.** She was a <u>tireless</u> worker for good causes. _____

Score on Exercise 2: _____

Exercise 3

Add *-ly* endings to the following words.

21. merry _____

22. busy _____

23. happy _____

24. clumsy _____

25. sloppy _____

Add *-ing* endings to the following words.

26. amaze _____

27. achieve _____

28. refine _____

29. convey _____

30. portray _____

Score on Exercise 3: _____

WRAP UP

Choose ten words from this lesson that you need to remember how to spell. Choose five and write them each five times on the lines below. Write the remaining five on index cards and add them to your Keeper List.

_____

_____

_____

_____

_____

ANSWERS

Exercise 1

1. intensity
2. receiving
3. enforcement
4. busily
5. chimneys
6. carrying
7. argument
8. pitiful
9. desirable
10. truly

Exercise 2

11. I, remedies
12. I, grievous
13. C
14. I, dizziness
15. C
16. C
17. I, unmistakable
18. C
19. I, mysteries
20. C

Exercise 3

21. merrily
22. busily
23. happily
24. clumsily
25. sloppily
26. amazing
27. achieving
28. refining
29. conveying
30. portraying

L·E·S·S·O·N 15

PROBLEM PLURALS

LESSON SUMMARY

This lesson shows you how to spell plurals, focusing particularly on trouble spots: words that end in long *o* and words that end in *f,* as well as the plurals of letters, numbers, and dates.

 ne of the difficulties of spelling in English is the making of plurals. Unfortunately, you can't always just add a simple letter *-s* to the end of the word to signal more than one.

WHEN TO USE *-S* OR *-ES* TO FORM PLURALS

The Rules

There are two simple rules that govern most plurals.

Most nouns add *-s* to make plurals.

If a noun ends in a *sibilant* sound *(s, ss, z, ch, x, sh)*, add *-es.*

Here are some examples:

cars	guesses	matches
computers	masses	blushes
skills	faxes	dishes
gases	indexes	flashes
businesses	churches	
dresses	lunches	

The Exception

Remember from the last lesson that when a word ends in a *y* preceded by a consonant, the *y* changes to *i* when you add *-es*.

fly—flies
mortuary—mortuaries
rally—rallies
tally—tallies

Memory Trick

Use this little ditty to help you remember the rule: "If you hear a sibilant *s*, the choice of a plural is likely *-es*."

In Context

Add *-s* or *-es* to the words in the sentences below.

1. He sent me two fax___ last night.

2. There were flash___ of lightening in the dark sky.

3. He struck several match___ before one finally caught fire.

4. You have two guess___ at the correct answer.

5. Spelling is one of the most helpful skill___ you can develop.

PLURALS FOR WORDS THAT END IN *O*

The Rule

There's just one quick rule that governs a few words ending in *o*.

If a final *o* follows another vowel, it takes *-s*.

Here are some examples:

patios	tattoos
radios	videos
studios	

The Exceptions

When the final *o* follows a consonant rather than a vowel, there's no rule to guide you in choosing *-s* or *-es*. You just have to learn the individual words.

These words form a plural with *-s* alone:

albinos	dynamos	silos
altos	grottos	sopranos
banjos	logos	tobaccos
broncos	pianos	

These words take *-es*:

embargoes	potatoes	vetoes
heroes	tomatoes	

When in doubt about whether to add -s or -es, look it up in the dictionary.

Memory Trick

Write each list on a card of a different color, or use a different color of ink. Read both cards five times each day for a week until you remember which card carried a particular word.

In Context

Add -s or -es to each underlined word below.

1. He peeled so many potato_____ in the army that he wouldn't eat French fries for a year.

2. The two soprano_____ gave a wonderful performance.

3. He wished there were more hero_____ in the world today.

4. The piano_____ were out of tune.

5. The farmers harvest their tomato_____ in the summer months.

PLURALS FOR WORDS THAT END IN *F*

Some words that end in *f* or *fe* just take -s to form the plural. Others change the *f* to *v* and add -es or -s. Unfortunately, there are no rules that can apply to this category of plurals. You just have to memorize them.

Here are some of the words that keep the final *f* and add -s:

beliefs	fifes	surfs
briefs	gulfs	turfs
chiefs	kerchiefs	
cuffs	proofs	

Here are some of the words that change the final *f* to *v* and take -es:

elves	loaves	wives
knives	selves	wolves
leaves	shelves	
lives	thieves	

Memory Trick

Use the same trick you used for final *o* words: Write each list in a different color and look at both lists several times a day until you know them.

In Context

Write the plural form of the words in the sentences below. If necessary, cross out the *f* and write *ves* instead.

1. He brought the proof_____ to the photographer.

2. The two thief_____ made off with many pieces of jewelry.

3. Their religious belief_____ helped to sustain them in their time of trouble.

4. The shelf_____ are full of interesting books.

5. The fresh green leaf_____ of the trees heralded the coming of spring.

PLURALS THAT DON'T USE *S* OR *ES*

There are a number of words in English that retain the plurals of the original language from which the word was borrowed.

From Old English

child-children
deer-deer
goose-geese
man-men
mouse-mice
ox-oxen
woman-women

From Latin

alumnus-alumni

curriculum-curricula

datum-data

fungus-fungi

medium-media

stratum-strata

From Greek

axis-axes

analysis-analyses

basis-bases

parenthesis-parentheses

oasis-oases

thesis-theses

Memory Trick

Most of the Old English plurals are part of your reading, speaking, and listening vocabularies. You simply have to learn the ones from Latin and Greek, though you can see that there are patterns that will help you. For instance, in Latin words, *-um* becomes *-a,* and in Greek words *-sis* becomes *-ses.* A good way to remember these plurals is by saying the words aloud, because for the most part they do change form and you may remember them more easily if you listen to the sound of the spelling.

In Context

Change the following words to plurals. Cross out any letters that change and write the new ones in the blanks.

1. The alumnus_____ of the college donated heavily to the building fund.

2. He didn't understand the datum_____ the study yielded.

3. The curriculum_____ of the three schools were very different.

4. The medium_____ were all fighting for interviews with the celebrity.

5. The woman_____ and child_____ were on their way to the station.

PLURALS FOR NUMBERS, LETTERS, AND DATES

The Rule

Numbers and letters usually form plurals by adding '*s* as if they were possessive.

Here are some examples of the rule:

Dot your *i*'s and cross your *t*'s.

How many 5's are in 25?

She is in her 20's.

The 1960's were a turbulent time.

Exceptions

Increasingly, people are dropping the apostrophe with numbers, including dates. If there's no possibility of confusion, it's usually OK to drop the apostrophe.

How many 5s are in 25?

She is in her 20s.

The 1960s were a turbulent time.

However, you should not drop the apostophe after letters, because people could get confused: Write *a*'s so people don't think you're writing *as.*

PRACTICE

Practice writing the plurals in Exercises 1 and 2 below. Check your answers at the end of the lesson. If you miss more than two in either exercise, complete Exercise 3 before going on to Test Practice.

Exercise 1

In the following paragraph change all underlined words to plurals.

On our trip west we had a chance to see wonderful scenery outside our **1)** window _____ including several country **2)** church _____ punctuating a plain dotted with grain **3)** silo _____ where the ranchers stored their harvests. We were invited to attend two **4)** rodeo _____ and watched **5)** cowboy _____ in their bright **6)** kerchief _____ roping the lively bucking **7)** bronco _____. The weather was good, though the heat brought out a lot of **8)** fly _____. One evening we went to a cowboy band where the music from the **9)** piano _____ and the **10)** banjo _____ kept up a foot-stomping beat until the small hours.

Score on Exercise 1: _____

Exercise 2

Write *C* in the first blank if the underlined word is spelled correctly and *I* if it is spelled incorrectly. If the word is misspelled, write it correctly in the blank after the sentence.

_____ **11.** We were washing <u>dishes</u> until nearly midnight. _____

_____ **12.** The <u>chiefs</u> were willing to meet with the rank and file in the department. _____

_____ **13.** The <u>thiefs</u> made off with all our luggage. _____

_____ **14.** The governor was considering three separate <u>vetos</u> for upcoming bills. _____

_____ **15.** The <u>sopranos</u> were the outstanding section in the chorus. _____

_____ **16.** The <u>tomatos</u> tasted wonderful. _____

_____ **17.** The movie <u>studios</u> were packed with visitors. _____

_____ **18.** He got three <u>Cs</u> on his report card. _____

_____ **19.** He attended <u>rally's</u> in support of his candidate. _____

_____ **20.** They bought several <u>loaves</u> of bread. _____

Score on Exercise 2: _____

Exercise 3

Write the plurals for the following words.

_____**21.** logo _____

_____**22.** crush _____

_____**23.** potato _____

_____**24.** I _____

_____**25.** fungus _____

_____**26.** loaf _____

_____**27.** dynamo _____

_____**28.** tax _____

_____**29.** glass _____

_____**30.** basis _____

Score on Exercise 3: _____

Test Practice

Circle the correct plural in each of the sentences below.

31. The artist had several (studios/studioes) where he worked.

32. We rented (videoes/videos) to watch last night.

33. The women wore brightly colored (kerchieves/kerchiefs) on their heads.

34. The nomads roamed the (oasisses/oases) of the desert.

35. He had to consult several (indexs/indexes) to find the information he needed.

36. The Challenger crew are remembered as (heros/heroes) by many Americans.

37. They drove the (oxes/oxen) over the rough prairie land.

38. The number of fatal car (crashs/crashes) has diminished this year.

39. The manufacturers are trying new strains of (tobaccoes/tobaccos) each year.

40. We planted a number of (hollies/hollys) in our yard this year.

WRAP UP

Choose ten words from this lesson and write five of them five times each on the blank lines. Then write the remaining five words on your Keeper List. You should have at least 30 words on your Keeper List by now. This would be a good time to have a friend quiz you on your list of spelling words.

_____

_____

_____

_____

_____

ANSWERS

Exercise 1	Exercise 2	Exercise 3	Test Practice
1. windows	11. C	21. logos	31. studios
2. churches	12. C	22. crushes	32. videos
3. silos	13. I, thieves	23. potatoes	33. kerchiefs
4. rodeos	14. I, vetoes	24. I's	34. oases
5. cowboys	15. C	25. fungi	35. indexes
6. kerchiefs	16. I, tomatoes	26. loaves	36. heroes
7. broncos	17. C	27. dynamos	37. oxen
8. flies	18. I, C's	28. taxes	38. crashes
9. pianos	19. I, rallies	29. glasses	39. tobaccos
10. banjos	20. C	30. bases	40. hollies

L · E · S · S · O · N
SNEAKY SUFFIXES
16

LESSON SUMMARY

This lesson helps you with spelling problems caused by suffixes. It shows you when to use *-ence* or *-ance*, *–ible* or *-able*, and other troublesome suffix pairs.

n Lesson 6 you learned that suffixes—word endings—often distinguish the part of speech of a word or its "job" in a sentence. When it comes to spelling, it's easy to become confused because several suffixes are similar in meaning but are spelled just a little differently.

WHEN TO USE *-ABLE* AND *-IBLE*

The Rules

There are several rules to guide you in choosing whether to use *-able* or *-ible*.

When to Use *-able*

If a word takes the *-ation* suffix, it usually takes *-able*.

    demonstration-demonstrable

    imagination-imaginable

    inflammation-inflammable

If a root word is complete in itself, it usually takes -able.

bear-bearable

drink-drinkable

laugh-laughable

read-readable

If a word ends in hard *c* or *g*, it will usually takes -able.

amicable

despicable

navigable

When to Use -ible

If a word takes the -ion suffix, it usually takes -ible.

collection-collectible

disruption-disruptible

division-divisible

If a word ends in -ss, it usually takes -ible.

accessible

admissible

irrepressible

permissible

If a root word is not a whole word, it usually takes -ible.

audible

horrible

responsible

terrible

visible

If a word ends in soft *c* or *g*, it usually takes -ible.

forcible

incorrigible

invincible

legible

reducible

reproducible

Memory Tricks

- There are about four times as many -*able* words in English as -*ible* words. If you are taking a guess, chances are -*able* is the correct choice.
- Think of a word in its noun form and use that to guide your choice of endings. For example, the noun form of the verb *convert* is *conversion*—which means that you should use -*ible*, according to the –*ion* rule.

The Exceptions

- The word *predict-prediction* does not follow the -*ion* rule and is changed to *predictable*.

WHEN TO USE –*ANT/-ANCY* AND -*ENT/-ENCY*

The Rules

The rules for using -*ant/-ance/-ancy* and -*ent/-ence/-ency* are only a few and don't cover all the cases. Here are a few guidelines:

Words with -*ant/-ance/-ancy* can be either nouns or adjectives.

Words with -*ent/-ence/-ency* can only be nouns.

Use -*ent/-ence/-ency* when the root word ends in:

sist or xist *(existence, persistence)*

soft *c* or *g* *(negligent, emergency)*

a vowel + *r* *(deference, reference)*

Here are some examples of words that take the *a* version of the ending:

abundant	inheritance	significance
brilliant	radiance	stimulant
elegance	relevance	tenancy
hesitancy	repentance	tolerance
ignorance	resistant	vacancy

Here are some examples of words that take the *e* version of the ending:

coherent	divergence	permanent
confident	frequent	precedent
consequence	indulgent	prominence
convenient	inference	reference
different	negligent	resident

The Exceptions

- *Resist* takes *-ant/-ance* even though it ends in *sist*: *resistant, resistance.*
- A few words end in *ense*. Most of these are fairly common and easy to remember: *expense, immense, nonsense, pretense, suspense.*

Memory Trick

If a root word contains an *a* as in *domin**a**te*, the likelihood is that it will take the *a* version of the ending: *dominance*. When in doubt, however, check the dictionary.

In Context

Use context to help you remember the rules. Circle the correct form of the word in each set of parentheses below.

1. She had an (abundance/abundence) of roses in her garden.

2. That was an (immence/immense) stretch of land before them.

3. The lawyer tried to prove (negligence/negligance) in the case.

4. He tried to overcome her (resistence/resistance) to changing jobs.

5. She was (repentent/repentant) for the way she treated her mother.

WHEN TO USE -ARY AND -ERY

You don't even need a rule to figure out whether to use *-ary* or *-ery*, because it's so simple. Only two common words end in *-ery: cemetery* and *stationery.* All other words take *-ary.* This includes the homophone of *stationery* (which means *writing paper*), *stationary* (which means *not moving*).

Here are some *-ary* words:

boundary	imaginary	secretary
contrary	library	solitary
dictionary	military	vocabulary
February	secondary	voluntary

WHEN TO USE -AL AND -EL

Again, there's no real rule for choosing between *-al* and *-el*, but fortunately there are relatively few *-el* words. If you have a basic acquaintance with the most common of *-el* words and remember that most words use *-al*, you will spell most of these words correctly.

Here are some of the most common *-el* words:

cancel	hovel	panel
channel	jewel	shovel
cruel	kennel	towel
drivel	model	travel
fuel	novel	tunnel

Here are a few of the many *-al* words:

accrual	lyrical	penal
choral	magical	personal
dismissal	mental	several
festival	moral	tribal
legal	neutral	
literal	oval	

PRACTICE

See if you can spot spelling errors and spell words correctly in the following exercises. Do Exercises 1 and 2 and check your answers at the end of the lesson. If you score less than 80 percent on either exercise, complete Exercise 3 for additional practice.

Exercise 1

Circle the correct spelling for the words in parentheses below.

1. The general thought the army was (invincibel/invincible).

2. He lived a (solitery/solitary) life after his wife died.

3. The building was not handicapped (accessable/accessible).

4. The bumper sticker said, "We're spending our children's (inheritence/inheritance)."

5. The class was restless as (dismissel/dismissal) time approached.

6. Theirs was an (amicable/amicabel) divorce with few hard feelings on either side.

7. He was a (prominant/prominent) attorney, well known throughout the city.

8. We left the dog in the (kennal/kennel) during our vacation.

9. He believed in a (literel/literal) interpretation of the Bible.

10. He made no (pretence/pretense) of being interested in sports.

Score on Exercise 1: _____

Exercise 2

Write *C* in the first blank if the underlined word is spelled correctly and *I* if it is spelled incorrectly. If the word is misspelled, write it correctly in the blank after the sentence.

_____11. He consulted several <u>referance</u> books in the <u>librery</u>. _____ _____

_____12. The doctor's handwriting was never very <u>legible</u>. _____

_____13. He said many of the bills were <u>un-collectible</u>. _____

_____14. The little girl had an <u>imaginery</u> friend called Sandy. _____

_____15. He made <u>frequent</u> visits to his elderly grandmother in England. _____

_____**16.** The villain was a <u>despicible</u> fiend, capable of doing great evil. _____

_____**17.** The oily rags in the garage turned out to be <u>inflammible</u>. _____

_____**18.** The politicians call for an end to welfare <u>dependancy</u>. _____

_____**19.** There were <u>visible</u> tracks along the snowy ridge. _____

_____**20.** He needed no chemical <u>stimulents</u> to keep him awake. _____

Score on Exercise 2: _____

Exercise 3

Fill in the missing letters in the words below to complete their spelling.

21. conveni__nt

22. diction__ry

23. imagin__ble

24. permiss__ble

25. indulg__nt

26. perman__nt

27. vac__ncy

28. chann__l

29. leg__l

30. aud__ble

Score on Exercise 3: _____

WRAP UP

Choose ten words from this lesson that you would like to learn to spell. Write each word five times on the blank lines. Then write the other five words on index cards to add to your Keeper List.

_____

_____

_____

_____

_____

ANSWERS

Exercise 1	Exercise 2	Exercise 3
1. invincible	11. I, reference, library	21. convenient
2. solitary	12. C	22. dictionary
3. accessible	13. C	23. imaginable
4. inheritance	14. I, imaginary	24. permissible
5. dismissal	15. C	25. indulgent
6. amicable	16. I, despicable	26. permanent
7. prominent	17. I, inflammable	27. vacancy
8. kennel	18. I, dependency	28. channel
9. literal	19. C	29. legal
10. pretense	20. I, stimulants	30. audible

L · E · S · S · O · N

SPELLING GLUE: PREFIXES, HYPHENS, AND COMPOUNDS

17

LESSON SUMMARY

This lesson deals with various ways of putting words and word parts together—prefixes, hyphenated words, and compound words—and shows you how to spell them.

esson 16 taught you how to spell suffixes—the endings of words. There are two other kinds of "add-ons" that good spellers need to know how to use. They are the prefixes that change or alter word meaning (see Lesson 5) and the hyphens that connect two words. Part of knowing how to use hyphens also involves knowing when *not* to use them.

PREFIXES

The Rule

Generally, when you add a prefix to a root word, neither the root nor the prefix changes spelling:

un- + prepared = unprepared
mal- + nutrition = malnutrition
sub- + traction = subtraction
mis- + informed = misinformed

This rule applies even when the root word begins with the same letter as the prefix. Generally you use both consonants. Here are some examples:

dissatisfied	irrational	transsexual
disservice	irregular	unnatural
illegible	misspelled	unnerved
illegitimate	misstep	

Memory Trick

Let your eye be your guide. Write the word without the double consonant and see what it looks like. If it looks funny, it is probably misspelled.

PREFIXES THAT CHANGE FORM

There are two sets of prefixes that can change form depending on the beginning of the word they are attached to.

Co-, col-, com-, and con-

The prefix *co-*, meaning *with*, is also written as *col-*, *com-*, and *con-*, depending on how the root begins. They all mean *with*; you just have to know which form to use. Your ear can guide you. You hear *cooperative*, not **com**operative or **col**operative. You hear *collateral*, not **com**lateral. You hear *compact*, not **con**pact. And so on.

Once you've heard the proper form of the prefix, the rule about not changing the spelling applies. Just add the prefix to the root word without changing the spelling.

Here are some examples of *co-*, *col-*, *com-*, and *con-* words:

cohabitation	commentator
cohesive	commercial
coworker	commitment
collaboration	congregation
collateral	contract
collating	contribute

In-, il-, im-, and ir-

The prefix *in-* means *not* or *the opposite of*. Again, the basic rule applies: You don't change the spelling of the root word when you add a prefix. Here are some examples:

infrequent
infertile
insubstantial

The prefix does change form, however. The forms *il-*, *im-*, and *ir-* are used with root words beginning with *l*, *m*, or *r*. The prefix changes in order to aid pronunication.

- Roots beginning with *l* take *il-*: *illogical* (not *inlogical*).
- Roots beginning with *m* take *im-*: *immoral* (not *inmoral*).
- Roots beginning with *r* take *ir-*: *irregular* (not *inregular*).

Your ear usually will tell you which form of the prefix to use.

SIMILAR PREFIXES THAT HAVE DIFFERENT MEANINGS
Pre-, pro-, and per-

In deciding to whether to use *pre-*, *pro-* or *per-*, the different meanings of the three prefixes should be your guide:

- *Pre-* means *before*: *prejudice*
- *Pro-* means *forward*: *project*
- *Per-* means *through*: *permeate*

Sound can also help you in choosing the right form if you are careful with pronunciation. Say, for instance, **pro**peller, not **per**peller.

Here are some *pro-*, *per-*, and *pre-* words.

proceed	percolator	prehensile
prohibit	permission	prehistoric
projection	perpetual	prenatal
proposition	persistence	prescribe

Anti- and *ante-*

Two more prefixes that can be confused in spelling are *anti-* and *ante-*. On this one, too, you have to go by the meaning of the prefix.

- *Anti-* means *against*: antibiotic (against biological organisms).
- *Ante-* means *before*: antebellum (before the war), anteroom (room before the room).

IN CONTEXT

Use context to help you learn the rules for prefixes. Circle the correctly spelled word in each of the following sentences.

1. The argument seemed ilogical/illogical to me.

2. He was busy collating/colating all the pages.

3. She was irreverent/ireverent in church today.

4. The comentator/commentator on TV summarized the news of the day.

5. They colaborated/collaborated on the project for school.

WHEN TO HYPHENATE

When you put words and word parts together, it's difficult to know when to leave the words separate, when to hyphenate, and when to put the words or word parts together into one new word. Do you write *co-dependent* or *codependent*? Do I have a *son in law* or a *son-in-law*? In both cases, it's the second choice.

There are at least eight rules for using hyphens to join words, often so that the joined words can perform a new function in the sentence.

- **Combine words with a hyphen to form an adjective when the adjective appears before a noun.**
  a well-heeled man
  a first-rate hotel
  a well-known actor

When the combination of words that makes an adjective appears *after* the noun, the combination is *not* hyphenated.

It's a job ill suited to his talents.
She is well regarded in the community.
The hotel is first rate.

- **Combine words with a hyphen when the words are used together as one part of speech.** This includes family relationships.
  editor-in-chief
  jack-of-all-trades
  maid-of-all-work
  mother-in-law
  runner-up
  sister-in-law

- **Use a hyphen before *elect* and after *vice, ex,* or *self*.**

  ex-President
  ex-teacher
  self-styled
  Senator-elect
  Vice-Admiral

- **Use a hyphen when joining a prefix to a root word that begins with the same letter that the prefix ends with, or in any other case where confusion might result.**

  bell-like
  co-owner
  pre-empt
  pre-existing
  re-enactment
  re-enlist

- **Use a hyphen when joining a prefix to a capitalized word.**

  mid-Atlantic
  pan-European
  post-Civil War
  trans-Siberian
  un-American

- **Use a hyphen to make compound numbers or fractions.**

  thirty-nine years
  one and two-thirds cups of broth

  Do not hypenate when the fraction is not a single adjective:

  one half of the country
  three fourths of the electorate

Also use a hyphen when you combine numbers with nouns.

  a class of six-year-olds
  a two-year term
  a twenty-five-cent fare

- **Use a hypen to form ethnic designations.**

  an African-American woman
  the Sino-Russian War
  the Austro-Hungarian Railroad

- **Use a hyphen to combine verbs and add-ons to form new nouns.** (*Add-ons* is a good example!)

  break-in
  cure-all
  cut-off
  lift-off
  play-off
  put-down
  stand-off

When Not to Hyphenate

Generally speaking, compound words are merely stuck together with no spelling change in either word. None of these words takes a hyphen:

airlift	carfare	railroad
boxcar	mailbox	sickroom
boyfriend	playpen	

Except for the cases noted above, prefixes are also joined directly to root words.

The best rule of thumb is this: If the phrase acts like an adjective, it probably needs a hyphen! If you want to put two words together and they don't seem to fit into any of these rules, the best strategy is to consult a dictionary.

In Context

Try using some hyphenated words in context. Add any needed hyphens in the sentences below. The answers are right after the sentences.

1. The insurance company would not waive the copayment because his illness was a preexisiting condition.

2. Two thirds of the people who answered the poll felt that the ex president made an excellent commander in chief.

3. My sister in law insists that the ill fated Knicks will still win the play offs.

4. A well known historian, a professor in his twenty seventh year at the college, was a preeminent authority on African American culture.

5. A prolife advocate was arrested for disributing antiabortion literature.

(**Answers: 1.** pre-existing; **2.** ex-president, commander-in-chief; **3.** sister-in-law, ill-fated, play-offs; **4.** well-known, twenty-seventh, pre-eminent, African-American; **5.** pro-life, anti-abortion)

PRACTICE

Complete Exercises 1 and 2 below. Check your answers at the end of the lesson. If you miss more than two questions on either exercise, complete Exercise 3 for reinforcement. Otherwise, go directly to Test Practice.

Exercise 1

Circle the correct spelling of the words in parentheses in the sentences below.

1. He was (unerved/unnerved) by being suddenly thrust into the spotlight.

2. He (mis-interpreted/misinterpreted) what she said about her (brother in law/brother-in-law) and his (fly by night/fly-by-night) business partners.

3. The (governor-elect/governor elect) was (disatisfied/dissatisfied) with his chief of staff and wanted to (replace/re-place) him when she took office.

4. It had been (fifty two/fifty-two) years since he had seen his old (comrade in arms/comrade-in-arms).

5. The two (ex servicemen/ex-servicemen) wanted to become (co-owners/coowners) of the new (three star/three-star) restaurant.

6. The two (co workers/coworkers) (colaborated/collaborated) on their (twice-weekly/twice weekly) report.

7. The director, (long established/long-established) as an innovator, decided to (reen-act/re-enact) the battle in front of the cameras.

8. The woman had (irational/irrational) fears about meeting her (long lost/long-lost) cousin.

9. We did him a (disservice/diservice) by (pre-moting/promoting) his brother ahead of him.

10. She waited in the (antiroom/anteroom) while her (coauthor/co-author) met with the (editor in chief/editor-in-chief).

Score on Exercise 1: _____

Exercise 2
Write *C* in the first blank if the underlined word is spelled correctly and *I* if it is spelled incorrectly. If the word is misspelled, write it correctly in the blank after the sentence.

_____ 11. He kept <u>irregular</u> hours and was often out until after midnight. _____

_____ 12. The bank wanted good <u>colateral</u> on its loan to the young couple. _____

_____ 13. The lines on the ancient vase were very <u>symetrical</u>. _____

_____ 14. The <u>stand up</u> comic played to a <u>well heeled</u> audience. _____ _____

_____ 15. He was the <u>runner up</u> in the contest and was invited to appear again. _____

_____ 16. The chocolate candy was <u>irresistible</u> to the toddler. _____

_____ 17. The <u>perjections</u> show that the sales figures were on target. _____

_____ 18. The class of <u>five-year-olds</u> enjoyed their trip to the aquarium. _____

_____ 19. He carved a scary <u>jack o lantern</u> at Halloween. _____

_____ 20. <u>Two thirds</u> of the employees were <u>laid off</u> from their jobs. _____ _____

Score on Exercise 2: _____

Exercise 3
The following words are spelled or hyphenated incorrectly. Write the correct spelling in the blank.

21. unAmerican _____

22. preempt _____

23. imoral _____

24. jack in the box _____

25. antebiotic _____

26. pre Civil War _____

27. Franco American _____

28. prehibit _____

29. pernatal _____

30. girl-friend _____

Score on Exercise 3: _____

Test Practice

Circle the correct spelling for the word that fits in the blank in each of the following sentences.

31. He _____ the word in class today.
   a. mispelled
   b. misspelled
   c. mis-spelled

32. He had a strong _____ to his job.
   a. comitment
   b. comittment
   c. commitment

33. She was _____ with the service at the restaurant.
   a. disatisfied
   b. dissatisfied
   c. disattisfied

34. The bank wanted _____ on its loan.
   a. collateral
   b. colateral
   c. co-lateral

35. There was an _____ quiet in the house.
   a. unatural
   b. un-natural
   c. unnatural

36. They met in the _____ to the office.
   a. antiroom
   b. anteroom
   c. auntiroom

37. It was hard to believe such an _____ story.
   a. illogical
   b. ilogical
   c. illogicle

38. She was accused of being an _____ woman.
   a. imoral
   b. imorral
   c. immoral

39. An _____ heartbeat kept him in the hospital.
   a. irregular
   b. iregular
   c. irreguler

40. The captain gave his permission to _____.
   a. procede
   b. proceed
   c. prosede

WRAP UP

Choose ten words from this lesson that you want to learn to spell. Write five of them five times each on the blank lines. Then write the remaining five words on index cards and add them to your Keeper List.

_____

_____

_____

_____

_____

ANSWERS

Exercise 1

 1. unnerved
 2. misinterpreted, brother-in-law, fly-by-night
 3. governor-elect, dissatisfied, replace
 4. fifty-two, comrade-in-arms
 5. ex-servicemen, co-owners, three-star
 6. coworkers, collaborated, twice-weekly
 7. long established, re-enact
 8. irrational, long-lost
 9. disservice, promoting
 10. anteroom, coauthor, editor-in-chief

Exercise 2

11. C
12. I, collateral
13. I, symmetrical
14. I, stand-up, well-heeled
15. I, runner-up
16. C
17. I, projections
18. C
19. I, jack-o-lantern
20. C

Exercise 3

21. un-American
22. pre-empt
23. immoral
24. jack-in-the-box
25. antibiotic
26. pre-Civil War
27. Franco-American
28. prohibit
29. prenatal
30. girlfriend

Test Practice

31. b
32. c
33. b
34. a
35. c
36. b
37. a
38. c
39. a
40. b

APOSTROPHES, ABBREVIATIONS, AND ACRONYMS

LESSON SUMMARY

The *A*'s have it! This lesson shows you when to use apostrophes—and when not to—and when and how to use abbreviations and acronyms.

postrophes are often misused, and knowing when to use them and when not to can be confusing. This lesson gives you a few simple rules to follow. After that is a section on abbreviations and acronyms, abbreviations that spell out individual words to represent entire phrases.

APOSTROPHES

Of all the punctuation marks, the apostrophe is the one most likely to be abused and confused. Fortunately, there are a few simple rules; if you follow them, you won't go wrong with apostrophes.

THE RULES

There are two rules about when to use apostrophes and one about when not to use them:

>   **Rule 1. Use an apostrophe to show possession:** Jack's book.

Rule 2. Use an apostrophe to make a contraction:
We don't like broccoli.

Rule 3. Do not use an apostrophe to make a plural:
I have two apples (not *apple's*).

See the table below for the rules on how to use apostrophes to form possessives.

Contractions

A contraction is formed by putting two words together and omitting one or more letters. Add an apostrophe to show that letters have been left out. Thus, "**We have** decided to move to Alaska" becomes, "**We've** decided to move to Alaska."

Here's a list of some of the most common contractions:

I will = I'll
he will = he'll
we will = we'll

it is = it's
she is = she's
you are = you're
they are = they're
we are = we're
cannot = can't
do not = don't
does not = doesn't
have not = haven't
should not = shouldn't
will not = won't

There are other ways in which an apostrophe can represent missing letters:

- In dialect: "I'm goin' down to the swimmin' hole," said the boy.
- When the letter *o* represents *of*: "Top o' the morning" or Mr. O'Reilly.

USING APOSTROPHES TO SHOW POSSESSION

Situation	Rule	Example
Singular noun	Add 's	Martha's Vineyard
Singular noun ending in ss	Add ' only	the hostess' home
Plural noun ending in s	Add ' only	the lawyers' bills
Plural noun not ending in s	Add 's	the Children's Museum, the men's clothes
Proper noun (name)	Add 's	Jenny's watch, Chris's car, Mrs. Jones's driveway
Singular indefinite pronoun	Add 's	one's only hope
Plural indefinite pronoun	Add ' only	all the others' votes
Compound noun	Add ' or 's after the final word	the men at arms' task, my mother-in-law's house
Joint possession	Add 's to the final name	Jim and Fred's Tackle Shop
Separate possession	Add 's after both names	Jim's and Fred's menus

The Exceptions

There is one exception to the rule about not using apostrophes to form plurals. As you saw in Lesson 15, you can use an apostrophe to make plurals of letters and numbers: I had three A's on my report card.

In Context

Practice using apostrophes in context by correcting the following sentences. The answers are right after the sentences.

1. Mrs. Clarks' store had been built in the 1970s.

2. Everyones lawn chair's were stored in John and Marys backyard.

3. They had gone to the ladies room to powder their nose's.

4. Wed rather have dinner at my mother-in-laws house next door.

5. Shouldnt he pick up his fax's before he goes home?

(**Answers: 1.** Clark's; **2.** Everyone's, chairs, Mary's; **3.** ladies', noses; **4.** We'd, mother-in-law's; **5.** Shouldn't, faxes)

ABBREVIATIONS

Many words and expressions in English are shortened by means of abbreviations. Though certain abbreviations are not usually used in formal writing, such as abbreviations for days of the week, they can be useful in less formal situations.

The Rule

Abbreviations are usually followed by periods.

See the table below for some examples of common abbreviations.

The Exceptions

- Don't use periods with the two-letter postal code abbreviations for states: CA, FL, IL, NJ, NY, TX, and so on.
- Don't use periods for initials representing a company or agency: FBI, CBS, NFL.
- Don't use periods after the letters in acronyms. (See below.)

COMMON ABBREVIATIONS

Type	Examples
Names of days	Sun., Mon., Tues., Wed., etc.
Names of months	Jan., Feb., Mar., Apr., etc.
Titles and degrees	Mr., Mrs., Ms., Esq., Dr., Hon., M.D., Ph.D., Ed.D.
Rank	Sgt., Capt., Maj., Col., Gen.
Business terms	C.O.D. (collect on delivery), Mfg. (Manufacturing), Inc. (Incorporated), Assn. (Association), Ltd. (Limited)

ACRONYMS

One of the ways that our language adds to its vocabulary is by creating acronyms. Acronyms are words made up of the first letters in a series of words or in a phrase. They differ from abbreviations or initials in that they make a word, which then represents the whole phrase. For example, the abbreviation *FBI* (Federal Bureau of Investigation) is pronounced *eff-bee-eye*, whereas the acronym *AIDS* (auto-immune deficiency syndrome) is pronounced as a word.

Here are some common acronyms and their derivations. Some of these acronyms have become so common as words that you may not even have known they were acronyms! Note that some acronyms are typically written in lowercase letters while others are all capital letters.

snafu = **s**ituation **n**ormal, **a**ll **f**ouled **up**

scuba = **s**elf-**c**ontained **u**nderwater **b**reathing **a**pparatus

yuppie = **y**oung **ur**ban **p**rofessional

dinks (a subset of yuppies) = **d**ouble **i**ncome couple, **n**o **k**ids

laser = **l**ight **a**mplification by **s**timulated **e**mission of **r**adiation

radar = **ra**dio **d**etecting **a**nd **r**anging

moped = **mo**tor **ped**al

WASP = **w**hite **A**nglo **S**axon **P**rotestant

WYSIWYG = **w**hat **you** **s**ee **is** **w**hat **you** **g**et (on a computer screen)

lifo = **l**ast **in**, **f**irst **o**ut (in employment)

There are also acronyms that are the names of organizations, scientific terms, or medical conditions that are too long to remember easily:

- **Groups**

  CORE = Council on Racial Equality

  UNICEF = United Nations International Children's Emergency Fund

  HUD = Housing and Urban Development, a government agency

  Fannie Mae = Federal National Mortgage Association

- **Medical terms**

  AIDS = auto-immune deficiency syndrome

  SIDS = sudden infant death syndrome

  CAT scan = computer assisted technology scan

- **Technological terms**

  REM = rapid eye movements (in sleep)

  RAM = random access memory (on a computer)

  COBOL = common business oriented (computer) language

A kind of reverse acronym is the word *emcee* which is derived from the initials M.C., for master of ceremonies.

PRACTICE

Complete exercises 1 and 2 below and check your answers at the end of the lesson. If you miss more than two questions in either exercise, complete Exercise 3 for additional practice.

Exercise 1

Correct the abbreviations and apostrophes in the following sentences.

1. Capt Meyerss ship was launched in the 1970s.

2. Tess dream was to earn three star's for her restaurant.

3. My mother-in-laws attorney's put the will in probate.

4. The National Womens Open brought players' from all over the world.

5. "Cant help lovin that man of mine," sang the shows lead, Betsy O Brien.

6. Everyones wish was for an end to that countries violence.

7. Shouldnt she have more than just Sids word that the house isnt very safe?

8. Shell want to know how the money got into the childrens' hands.

9. Joe and Harrys music could be heard on Lindas tape player.

10. Carols and Judys dress's were hanging on the seamstress door.

Score on Exercise 1: _____

Exercise 2

Use the list of acronyms in this lesson to complete the following sentences.

11. My doctor ordered a _____ to determine if I needed surgery.

12. If I needed a mortgage, I might apply for one through _____.

13. Many dollars from _____ have contributed to the aid of children all over the world.

14. If I needed a computer language for my business I would probably need _____.

15. Some feminists object to the teaching of so many works by _____ in our liberal arts colleges and so few by women and minority authors.

16. As usual, some _____ at the Motor Vehicle Bureau kept me waiting for an hour.

17. If I plan to go diving I should take my _____ gear.

18. The air traffic controller scanned the _____ screen to search for planes.

19. The plague of our century is probably the _____ epidemic.

20. Some young people are rejecting the _____ lifestyle in favor of a more relaxed and less materialistic way of life.

Score on Exercise 2: _____

Exercise 3

Circle the correct term in each sentence below.

21. I will have two (week's/weeks') vacation in (N.O.V./Nov.) this year.

22. Gen. (Jone's/Jones's) order was to leave on (Sun./Sund.)

23. My attorney is addressed as James Olsen, (Esqu./Esq.)

24. (Russ's/Russ') aunt had (lasar/laser) surgery to correct her cataracts.

25. My letter to my professor was addressed, Mary Stevens, (PHD./Ph.D.)

26. (Les's and Larry's/Les and Larry's) mopeds were parked outside.

27. The ancient Greeks worshiped at the (goddess'/goddess's) shrine every spring.

28. Doctors in sleep disorder clinics study patients' (REM/R.E.M.) sleep.

29. It was (their/they're) decision to move to (N.Y./NY) over the summer.

30. (Maj./Mjr.) Clark was the (emcee/emmcee) on the USO tour this year.

Score on Exercise 3: _____

WRAP UP

Choose ten words from this lesson that are new or unfamiliar. Write five of them in original sentences below. Write the other five words on index cards to add to your Keeper List.

_____

_____

_____

_____

_____

Study Skills

If you can work with a study buddy or have someone help you review your work in this book, here are some suggestions for working together:

- Brainstorm with your partner about abbreviations or acronyms that are new to you. See if you can think of five more that you can add to the list in this lesson.

- Play "Jeopardy" with words. You give a definition and your partner gives you the word in a question. For example, your definition might be, "A word that means a person who guarantees business to a company." The answer is, "What is a rainmaker?" (See Lesson 19.)

- Choose ten words you really want to remember. Write each word on an index card and then make a duplicate set so you can play Concentration. Put all the cards face down. Take turns turning over two cards at a time to see if you have a "match." This works even better if you have the word on one card and the definition on the other.

- Choose six words and write them on index cards. Place them facing up on the table. Close your eyes. Let your partner take one away. See if you can remember the missing word. If you can't remember, let your partner give you a definition to remind you. Take turns doing this. Add more cards if you want more of a challenge.

- Ask your partner to spell the words aloud. Then you spell the words aloud. Your ear will help you to remember the spelling of a difficult word.

ANSWERS

Exercise 1

1. Capt., Meyers's
2. Tess', stars
3. mother-in-law's, attorneys
4. Women's, players
5. Can't, lovin', show's, O'Brien
6. Everyone's, country's
7. Shouldn't, Sid's, isn't
8. She'll, children's
9. Harry's, Linda's
10. Carol's, Judy's, dresses, seamstress'

Exercise 2

11. CAT scan
12. Fannie Mae
13. UNICEF
14. COBOL
15. WASPS
16. snafu
17. scuba
18. radar
19. AIDS
20. yuppie

Exercise 3

21. weeks', Nov.
22. Jones's, Sun.
23. Esq.
24. Russ's, laser
25. Ph.D.
26. Les's and Larry's
27. goddess'
28. REM
29. their, NY
30. Maj., emcee

L·E·S·S·O·N 19

BRAVE NEW WORDS: LEARNING AND SPELLING EMERGING VOCABULARY

LESSON SUMMARY

Today's lesson shows you how to learn both the meaning and the spelling of new words, concentrating on new and emerging vocabulary in science and technology, business, politics, society, and the media.

English is a difficult language to read and spell because of its odd phonetic system and complicated spelling patterns. One of the wonderful things about the language, however, is that it is flexible. English is constantly adding new words, borrowing terms from technology, the arts, or business. As an individual, you can be as creative about summoning new words into your reading, speaking, and listening vocabularies as our society as a whole is about admitting such new words in the first place.

This lesson will explore some of the newer words and expressions that have enriched our language and teach you how to add other such words to your vocabulary as they develop.

NEW AND EMERGING VOCABULARY WORDS

Here are a few examples of words that have recently entered our language. How many do you know by sight or sound?

From Science and Technology

ballistic	global warming
biosphere	greenhouse effect
boot up	meltdown
China syndrome	in-vitro fertilization
clone	narrowcasting
cryogenics	surrogate mothers
glitch	

From Business and Industry

cash cow	junk bonds
disincentives	mommy track
downsizing	networking
fast track	outsourcing
flextime	Peter Principle
glass ceiling	rainmaker
golden parachute	upscale
headhunter	worst case scenario
human resources	

From Politics, Society, and the Media

baby boomers	rustbelt
co-parenting	significant other
Generation X	spa cuisine
gentrification	spin doctors
hip-hop	stonewall
palimony	sunbelt
policy wonk	tabloid television
prequel	

HOW NEW WORDS ARE CREATED

Words like the ones above arise out of a need—the need to describe something that didn't exist or wasn't common before. We create words to fit a new situation. Here's how:

- We describe events or trends in colorful, creative ways. For example, if women seem limited in their ability to rise in the corporate world because they encounter barriers to promotion that they can't see, we call that situation a *glass ceiling*.
- We blend words to make new ones. Here are some words made up of two words:
    brunch (breakfast and lunch)
    camcorder (camera recorder)
    cremains (remains after cremation)
    docudrama (documentary drama)
    infomercial (informational commercial)
    kidvid (kids' video)
    pixel (picture element)
    simulcast (simultaneous broadcast)
    sitcom (situation comedy)
    smog (smoke and fog)
- We make words from brand names, which come to represent the product itself, regardless of the manufacturer. Eventually, these words drop their capital letters, as has happened or is happening to these brand names:

band-aid	scotch tape
crayolas	thermos
jello	xerox
kleenex	

- We create new forms based on historical events. For instance, since the scandal in the 1970s regarding the break-in at the Watergate Hotel, the media have tended to refer in a humorous way to any major scandal by adding the word "–gate" to the term. For example, "Pearly-gate" referred to the downfall of some prominent religious leaders, while "Whitewater-gate" has been used to refer to President Clinton's involvement in dubious investments. Note that such words generally are hyphenated.

SPELLING HINTS FOR NEW AND EMERGING VOCABULARY

In most cases, new terms are fairly easy to spell if you remember the spelling of the individual components of the word. For example, the blended word *stagflation*, which refers to high prices in a sluggish economy, is taken from the words *stagnant* and *inflation*. Knowing the spellings of both of these words means you can spell the new term as well.

For Non-native Speakers of English (and Others)

There are two major difficulties in learning English vocabulary in adulthood. The first is idiomatic expressions. *Idioms* are expressions in a language that don't conform to strict grammatical rules but are understood by those who speak the language. For example, "I am *on* the phone" doesn't mean that someone is sitting on the receiver but that someone is *using* the phone.

New expressions in the language are often idioms. *Spin doctors* is a good example of an idiom. It has nothing to do with either spinning or doctors. It means that advisors try to "doctor" their candidate's speech by putting a favorable interpretation (or "spin") on what he or she said. "Spin" in this connection refers to the act of directing a ball in a certain direction by means of a particular thrust.

A second difficulty arises when we realize that words have both *denotations*, literal meanings such as you would find in a dictionary, and *connotations*, meanings that are associated with words based on how they are used. An easy way to think of connotations is to think of them as "flavors" of words. Some words have pleasant associations, while others have less pleasant connotations. Take, for example, words associated with the idea of thinness. Words such as *slim*, *lithe*, and *slender* have pleasant connotations, while *skinny*, *scrawny*, and *skeletal*—though they still mean *thin*—have unpleasant connotations. The different "flavors" of the words give different meanings to a sentence.

Thus, the word *yuppie* means more than just its acronym would suggest—young adults working in white collar jobs in a city. It has come to be associated with a kind of lifestyle in which making money and buying a lot of unnecessary consumer goods is the most important value. It has a less pleasant connotation than you would think if you went strictly by the dictionary definition.

For these reasons, non-native speakers of English should talk regularly with native English speakers about the meanings of idioms and the interpretation of some vocabulary words. Often the dictionary is less helpful than it would seem.

Here are some spelling hints you can use for new words:

- Look for **compounds:** sunbelt, rustbelt, rain-maker, downsizing, meltdown, headhunter.
- Look for familiar **prefixes:** *dis*incentive, *co*-parenting, *bio*sphere, *pre*quel.
- Break words into **syllables:** gen-tri-fi-ca-tion, sur-ro-gate.

HOW TO LEARN NEW TERMS

Since the language is continually adding new terms and phrases, learning new vocabulary is a lifelong task. Here are some general strategies for learning emerging vocabulary words:

- Be sensitive to the language you hear around you. When you hear the news or read the newspaper, write down new or unfamiliar words and phrases.
- Use what you already know to help you figure out what new terms mean. Most *neologisms,* or new words and expressions, have pretty obvious meanings because they were created for specific needs.

New Terms Exercise

Test your strategies out on the some of the words and phrases listed above. Match the words and phrases in the first column with their definitions in the second column. Answers are at the end of the lesson.

_____ **1.** surrogate mothers

_____ **2.** headhunter

_____ **3.** palimony

_____ **4.** rustbelt

_____ **5.** upscale

_____ **6.** prequel

_____ **7.** baby boomers

_____ **8.** Generation X

_____ **9.** cash cow

_____ **10.** significant other

a. the post-World War II generation

b. a story that tells what happened before another story

c. an area characterized by abandoned factories and heavy industries

d. mothers who bear children for other women

e. high priced goods and services, or the people who use them

f. money to support a partner in an unmarried relationship after the relationship is over

g. a business or investment made to yield immediate profit

h. an employment agency

i. a person in a committed but unmarried relationship

j. young people in their 20s

PRACTICE

Complete Exercises 1 and 2 below for practice in using some of these new terms. Check your answers at the end of the lesson. If you miss more than two in either exercise, complete Exercise 3 for more practice.

Exercise 1

From the context cues given below, choose the term from the word bank that fits each sentence.

Word Bank

cryogenics	human resources
disincentives	Peter Principle
downsizing	policy wonk
fast track	spin doctors
global warming	tabloid television
greenhouse effect	worst case scenario

1. The study of the physics of very low temperatures and their effects on the body is called _____.

2. An executive would be alarmed to learn that the _____ is actually about to happen.

3. We don't like to say we are firing people; we prefer to say we are _____ our staff.

4. When someone rises in his company until he reaches the level of his own incompetence, we say he is an example of the _____.

5. After a politician speaks out on an issue, the _____ come on the air to put the most favorable interpretation on his remarks.

6. When we look for a job we inquire at the _____ department, once called "personnel."

7. If you want to hear about the seamy side of life, you can find all you want on _____, which specializes in sensational stories.

8. If you are headed for rapid promotion and quick success you are on the _____.

9. Scientists warn that increased carbon dioxide emissions will create a _____, which could raise temperatures worldwide and result in _____.

10. An expert or advisor to politicians regarding issues of public concern is sometimes called a _____.

Score on Exercise 1: _____ (out of 11)

Exercise 2

Choose the blended word or brand name that fits in each sentence below.

11. If I wanted to photocopy something I would _____ it.

12. If I wanted to watch an amusing program with a continuing story line, I would watch my favorite _____.

13. A program on television that featured new cosmetics might be an _____.

14. If the air in my town is polluted, I can look out my window and see a haze of _____.

15. If I wanted a late morning meal, I might have _____.

16. If I wanted to wrap a package, I would need _____ to secure the paper.

17. If I want to make a film of my child's birthday party, I could use a _____.

18. If I want to watch a concert on television and listen to it on the radio at the same time, it needs to be _____.

19. If I want to serve a molded dessert, I would probably use _____.

20. People sometimes scatter the ashes or _____ of a loved one in a special place.

Score on Exercise 2: _____

Exercise 3

Mark the following statements as true or false according to the meaning of the underlined word or phrase.

_____21. Hip-hop is a contemporary music style.

_____22. A docudrama is an imaginative look at a real situation.

_____23. A child would use crayolas to catch fish.

_____24. A person who goes ballistic is calm and assured.

_____25. The process by which people make connections for the purpose of doing business is called networking.

_____26. In-vitro fertilization takes place outside the mother's body.

_____27. Lots of people retire to the sunbelt.

_____28. An exact genetic duplication is a biosphere.

_____29. Spa cuisine includes menus for dieters.

_____30. When a company hires an outside party to provide certain materials or services, that company is outsourcing.

Score on Exercise 3: _____

WRAP UP

Choose ten words from today's lesson that are new or unfamiliar to you. Choose five of them, and write each in a sentence below. Then write the other five on index cards and add them to your Keeper List.

_____

_____

_____

_____

ANSWERS

New Terms Exercise

1. d
2. h
3. f
4. c
5. e
6. b
7. a
8. j
9. g
10. i

Exercise 1

1. cryogenics
2. worst case scenario
3. downsizing
4. Peter Principle
5. spin doctors
6. human resources
7. tabloid television
8. fast track
9. greenhouse effect, global warming
10. policy wonk

Exercise 2

11. xerox
12. sitcom
13. infomercial
14. smog
15. brunch
16. scotch tape
17. camcorder
18. simulcast
19. jello
20. cremains

Exercise 3

21. true
22. true
23. false
24. false
25. true
26. true
27. true
28. false
29. true
30. true

L · E · S · S · O · N 20

REVIEW: VOCABULARY AND SPELLING FOR ADULT LEARNERS

LESSON SUMMARY

This lesson completes your study of vocabulary and spelling by putting the two together. It shows you how the spelling lessons you learned are used in some of the vocabulary from Lessons 1–10. It contains a list of traditional spelling "demons"—words that most people make the same mistakes with over and over—and shows you how to conquer them, this time for good. You'll also learn how to eliminate the Top Ten spelling and usage errors from your writing.

If you are a working adult and have spent about twenty minutes each work day going through these lessons, it took you about a month to complete this book. By now the book should look pretty well lived in. This final lesson pulls the vocabulary and spelling sections together to show you how much you've learned.

SPELLING YOUR VOCABULARY

Below are several of the spelling strategies that you studied in Lessons 11–18 with examples of words from the vocabulary of Lessons 1–10.

Vowel Combinations

Remember the vowel combinations you studied in Lesson 12? Here are some vocabulary words that follow—or are exceptions to—those rules.

- **Villain** follows the *ai* rule—*ai* sounds like *uh.*
- **Naive** doesn't follow the *ai* rule. It sounds more or less the way it did in its original language, French, so it has two syllables: *nah-EEVE.* In **malaise,** on the other hand, *ai* sounds like long *a.*
- **Depreciation, agrarian, jovial,** and **draconian** follow the *ia* rule—the two letters are sounded separately.
- **Revenue** has an *oo* sound at the end, signaled by the silent final *e.*
- **Fluctuate** is an example of a word that has what looks like a vowel combination but isn't. Both the *u* and the *a* are sounded in separate syllables: *FLUC-tyoo-ate.*

Silent Consonants

Here are some of the vocabulary words you learned that have silent consonants.

- **Malign** has a silent *g.* A good way to remember this is to think of the noun form, *malignancy.* You hear the *g* in *malignancy,* so this will help you remember to spell *malign* with the *g.*
- **Debut, faux pas, précis, coup d'etat, potpourri** all have silent consonants at the end of a syllable. These words are French and retain some of their original pronunciation. There's really no rule for pronouncing words from other languages; you just have to find ways of remembering them.

Words With *C, G,* and *K*

When *c* and *g* are followed by *e, i,* or *y,* they have a soft sound: *c* sounds like *s* and *g* sounds like *j.* Here are some examples of words from the vocabulary lessons that have soft *c* and *g* sounds:

cynical	precedent
genocide	précis
gerrymander	secession
incisive	tangential

On the other hand, when *c* and *g* are followed by other letters, they have hard sounds: *c* sounds like *k* and *g* sounds like *g* as in *great.* Examples from the vocabulary lessons include *prosecution* and *jargon.*

Words That End in Y

Some of the vocabulary words from this book that end in the letter *y* are:

accessory	equity
amnesty	fidelity
antipathy	inventory
apathy	parity
controversy	philanthropy
currency	subsidy

These words are all nouns. A verb that ends in *y* is *rectify.*

When you want to make plurals of these words, change the *y* to *i* and add *-es.* Choose four of the words above and write them as plurals below.

_____

_____

Words With Significant Endings

When you know the spellings of word parts—roots, prefixes, or suffixes—you can usually spell the whole word, because those elements rarely change much when they are put together. The table below shows some vocabulary words that use the suffixes you have studied.

Compound Words and Hyphenated Words

Here are some of the compound words you have learned, as well as two hyphenated terms:

downsizing	upscale
headhunter	voicemail
network	website
software	e-mail
spreadsheet	on-line

SPELLING DEMONS

Spelling "demons" have plagued most of us since elementary school. Some are words that don't fit various spelling or grammar rules, so you have to learn them by sight. Some are just plain hard to remember.

Below are ten words you learned in this book that are fairly common but difficult to spell:

accessory	deferment
belligerent	entrepreneur
beneficiary	harassment
bourgeoise	mediocre
ceiling	repertoire
cynical	thorough

Choose four of your own spelling demons. You might choose some of the words listed above, words from your Keeper List, other words from this book, or your own personal "tough words," that you would like to make sure you know. Write your words in the spaces below, and then write them on index cards and add them to your Keeper List.

_____

_____

SUFFIXES

Suffix	Examples	Suffix	Examples
-able	biodegradable, laudable	–less	relentless
–al	fiscal, jovial, nominal	–ment	impediment, deferment, entitlement, harassment, impediment
–ant/-ance/-ent	exorbitant, remittance, antecedent, incumbent, malevolent	–ous	conspicuous, copious, gregarious, tenacious
–ic	cryptic, erotic, forensic, narcissistic, quixotic, stoic, titanic	–tion	arbitration, deposition, depreciation, discrimination, mutation, prosecution

There are many other words in general use whose spelling is hard to remember. Appendix B includes a list of such words. Follow the directions for study in Appendix B. Work with a partner to learn the words until their spelling becomes second nature to you.

COMMON SPELLING AND USAGE ERRORS

Listed below are the Top Ten Absolute No-No's of writing. Mistakes with these words are common but stick out like a sore thumb. Conquer these Top Ten now and they'll never show up to mar your writing again.

The Top Ten Absolute No-No's of Writing

1. **Don't confuse *its* and *it's*.**
   Its is a possessive pronoun: A dog knows its owner.
   It's is a contraction for *it is:* It's going to rain.

2. **Don't confuse *their*, *there*, and *they're*.**
   Their is a possessive pronoun: They went to their homes.
   There is an adverb of place: Sit down over there.
   They're is a contraction for *they are:* They're going home soon.

3. **Don't confuse *two*, *too*, and *to*.**
   Two is a number: She has two college degrees.
   Too means *also:* She had a new car, too.
   To is a preposition: She wanted to go home earlier.

4. **Don't write *try and, be sure and, come and*.**
   These phrases take *to:* Try to understand my point of view and be sure to explain it to your friend. Then come to see me.

5. **Don't write *should of, could of, must of, would of*.**
   The proper forms are *should have, could have, must have, would have:* I could have gone to the movies. I should have brought a handkerchief.

6. **Don't write *suppose to* or *use to*.**
   The proper forms are *supposed to* and *used to:* I was supposed to go to college but I couldn't get used to being away from home.

7. **Don't confuse *differ from* and *differ with*.**
   Differ from means *unlike:* Her tests differ from everyone else's exams.
   Differ with means *disagree:* I differ with him on the issue of capital punishment.

8. **Don't confuse *amount* and *number*, *less* and *fewer*.**
   Use *amount* with words that are singular: There was a large amount of cash missing from the drawer.
   Use *number* with words that are plural: There is a large number of ten dollar bills missing from her wallet.
   Use *less* with words that are singular: He has less money than he had last week.
   Use *fewer* with words that are plural: He has fewer ways of spending his money.

9. **Don't confuse *compare with* and *compare to*.**
   Compare with means to look at ways things are similar: She never wanted to compare her daughter *with* her son.
   Compare to means to represent as being alike: As a singer he was being compared *to* Elvis Presley.

10. **Never use the word orientate.** It doesn't exist. The word you want is *orient:* I wanted to orient myself in my new job before I moved to a new apartment.

SPELLING MUSTS

In filling out applications and other important documents, you must know how to spell all the important words and phrases. Especially on an application or resume, where you are making your first impression on a potential employer, you want to make sure that your words appear "well groomed."

Don't ever try to fill out forms without knowing the correct spelling of:

- Your street address. Since you may also be asked for previous addresses, you should know and be able to spell your previous addresses for the last five years.
- The names and titles of people you are using as references.
- The businesses where you have worked.
- Positions you have held or titles you have had. Examples might include plant manager, site super-visor (never sight supervisor!), foreman, shop steward, clerk, and so on.

- The basic information an application might require. Below are some terms that are commonly used in applications and other forms adults use in the workplace.

applicant	personnel
available	promotion
benefits	references
cashier	retail
certificate	superintendent
clerical	union
diploma	wholesale
maintenance	

PRACTICE

Complete Exercises 1 and 2 below and check your answers at the end of the lesson. If you score less than 80 percent on either exercise, complete Exercise 3 for additional practice. Even if you score 80 percent or more, you might enjoy doing Exercise 3.

Application Tip

Keep vital information such as your former addresses and work history, as well as any employment terms you might need on an application, in a small notebook or on a card you can carry in your purse or wallet. That way you'll be sure to have it even if you unexpectedly have to fill out an application or other form.

If you can take an application home to fill it out, make a couple of photocopies before you start so that you can redo any part that needs corrections or gets messy while you are working on it.

Exercise 1

Circle the correct spelling for the words below.

1. a. coppious
   b. copius
   c. copious
   d. copeous

2. a. depresheashun
   b. deprecation
   c. deppreciation
   d. depreciation

3. a. exorbitant
   b. ex-orbitant
   c. exourbitant
   d. exorbitent

4. a. entitlment
   b. entitelment
   c. entitlement
   d. entitalment

5. a. narcissitik
   b. narcisistic
   c. narcississtic
   d. narcissistic

6. a. laudeble
   b. laudible
   c. laudable
   d. laudebel

7. a. anmesty
   b. amnesty
   c. amnisty
   d. anmusty

8. a. currensy
   b. currincy
   c. curency
   d. currency

9. a. controversy
   b. controversie
   c. contraversy
   d. contriversy

10. a. parety
    b. parity
    c. paratie
    d. parrity

Score on Exercise 1: _____

Exercise 2

Circle the correct word or phrase in each sentence below:

11. (Its/It's) not going to be easy to go back to work.

12. They went to the bank to take (there/their they're) money out of the money market account.

13. We (should of/should have) gone to Florida for the winter.

14. It takes time to get (orientated/oriented) to a new neighborhood.

15. You should (try and/try to) get some rest before the trip.

16. Don't be (to/too/two) upset over the baseball standings.

17. She had saved a large (number/amount) of antique dolls from her mother's collection.

18. She was (supposed to/suppose to) get a promotion in her job, but it fell through.

19. She (differed with/differed from) her sister with regard to gun control.

20. Her craftsmanship was (compared to/compared with) that of the Williamsburg artists.

Score on Exercise 2: _____

Exercise 3

Unscramble these words. They all appear in this lesson.

21. calfis _____

22. diancrona _____

23. patithnay _____

24. lompida _____

25. vijola _____

26. teroci _____

27. tenkrow _____

28. sonperlen _____

29. venmalotel _____

30. sicrofen _____

WRAP UP

Congratulations! You've finished this book, and if you've followed its advice about making a Keeper List, you've added a hundred words or more to your vocabulary of correctly spelled words. You're better prepared than you were before you started this book to meet your goals, whether they include doing well on a test, getting better at your job or getting a new job, or just impressing the people you speak and write to as a well-educated person.

Don't stop now. If you're preparing for an exam, you'll want to turn to Appendix A, which tells you everything you need to know about preparing for and taking a standardized test.

Learning vocabulary and spelling is a lifelong process. See Appendix A for additional tips and resources for continuing to improve your word power.

ANSWERS

Exercise 1	Exercise 2	Exercise 3
1. c	11. It's	21. fiscal
2. d	12. their	22. draconian
3. a	13. should have	23. antipathy
4. c	14. oriented	24. diploma
5. d	15. try to	25. jovial
6. c	16. too	26. erotic
7. b	17. number	27. network
8. d	18. supposed to	28. personnel
9. a	19. differed with	29. malevolent
10. b	20. compared to	30. forensic

PREPARING FOR A STANDARDIZED TEST

A standardized test is nothing to fear. Many people clutch and worry about a testing situation, but you're much better off taking that nervous energy and turning it into something positive that will help you do well on your test rather than inhibit your testing ability. The following pages include valuable tips for combating test anxiety, that sinking or blank feeling some people get as they begin a test or encounter a difficult question. Next, you will find valuable tips for using your time wisely and for avoiding errors in a testing situation. Finally, you will see a plan for preparing in the days before the test, a plan for the test day, and a great suggestion for an after-test activity.

COMBATING TEST ANXIETY

Knowing what to expect and being prepared for it is the best defense against test anxiety, that worrisome feeling that keeps you from doing your best. Practice and preparation keeps you from succumbing to that feeling.

Nevertheless, even the brightest, most well-prepared test takers may suffer from occasional bouts of test anxiety. But don't worry; you can overcome it.

Take the Test One Question at a Time

Focus all of your attention on the one question you're answering. Block out any thoughts about questions you've already read or concerns about what's coming next. Concentrate your thinking where it will do the most good—on the question you're answering.

Develop a Positive Attitude

Keep reminding yourself that you're prepared. The fact that you're reading this book means that you're better prepared than most of the others who are taking the test. Remember, it's only a test, and you're going to do your best. That's all anyone can ask of you. If that nagging drill sergeant voice inside your head starts sending negative messages, combat them with positive ones of your own.

- "I'm doing just fine."
- "I've prepared for this test."
- "I know exactly what to do."
- "I know I can get the score I'm shooting for."

You get the idea. Remember to drown out negative messages with positive ones of your own.

If You Lose Your Concentration

Don't worry about it! It's normal. During a long test it happens to everyone. When your mind is stressed or overexerted, it takes a break whether you want it to or not. It's easy to get your concentration back if you simply acknowledge the fact that you've lost it and take a quick break. You brain needs very little time (seconds really) to rest.

Put your pencil down and close your eyes. Take a few deep breaths and listen to the sound of your breathing. The ten seconds or so that this takes is really all the time your brain needs to relax and get ready to focus again.

Try this technique several times in the days before the test when you feel stressed. The more you practice, the better it will work for you on the day of the test.

If You Freeze Before or During the Test

Don't worry about a question that stumps you even though you're sure you know the answer. Mark it and go on to the next question. You can come back to the "stumper" later. Try to put it out of your mind completely until you come back to it. Just let your subconscious mind chew on the question while your conscious mind focuses on the other items (one a time—of course). Chances are, the memory block will be gone by the time you return to the question.

If you freeze before you ever begin the test, here's what to do.

1. Take a little time to look over the test.
2. Read a few of the questions.
3. Decide which ones are the easiest and start there.
4. Before long, you'll be "in the groove."

TIME STRATEGIES

Pace Yourself

The most important time strategy is pacing yourself. Before you begin, take just a few seconds to survey the test, making note of the number of questions and of the sections that look easier than the rest. Rough out a time schedule based upon the amount of time available to you. Mark the halfway point on your test and make a note beside that mark of what the time will be when the testing period is half over.

Keep Moving

Once you begin the test, keep moving. If you work slowly in an attempt to make fewer mistakes, your mind will become bored and begin to wander. You'll end up making far more mistakes if you're not concentrating.

As long as we're talking about mistakes, don't stop for difficult questions. Skip them and move on. You can come back to them later if you have time. A question that takes you five seconds to answer counts as much as one that takes you several minutes, so pick up the easy points first. Besides, answering the easier questions first helps to build your confidence and gets you in the testing groove. Who knows? As you go through the test, you may even stumble across some relevant information to help you answer those tough questions.

Don't Rush

Keep moving, but don't rush. Think of your mind as a seesaw. On one side is your emotional energy. On the other side is your intellectual energy. When your emotional energy is high, your intellectual capacity is low. Remember how difficult it is to reason with someone when you're angry? On the other hand, when your intellectual energy is high, your emotional energy is low. Rushing raises your emotional energy. Remember the last time you were late for work? All that rushing around causes you to forget important things—like your lunch. Move quickly to keep your mind from wandering, but don't rush and get yourself flustered.

Check Yourself

Check yourself at the halfway mark. If you're a little ahead, you know you're on track and may even have a little time left to check your work. If you're a little behind, you have several choices. You can pick up the pace a little, but do this only if you can do it comfortably. Remember—**don't rush!** You can also skip around in the remaining portion of the test to pick up as many easy points as possible. This strategy has one drawback, however. If you are marking a bubble-style answer sheet, and you put the right answers in the wrong bubbles—they're wrong. So pay close attention to the question numbers if you decide to do this.

AVOIDING ERRORS

When you take the test, you want to make as few errors as possible in the questions you answer. Here are a few tactics to keep in mind.

Control Yourself

Remember the comparison between your mind and a seesaw that you read about a few paragraphs ago?

Keeping your emotional energy low and your intellectual energy high is the best way to avoid mistakes. If you feel stressed or worried, stop for a few seconds. Acknowledge the feeling (Hmmm! I'm feeling a little pressure here!), take a few deep breaths, and send yourself a few positive messages. This relieves your emotional anxiety and boosts your intellectual capacity.

Directions

In many standardized testing situations, a proctor reads the instructions aloud. Make certain you understand what is expected. If you don't, **ask.** Listen carefully for instructions about how to answer the questions and make certain you know how much time you have to complete the task. Write the time on your test if you don't already know how long you have to take the test. If you miss this vital information, **ask for it.** You need it to do well on your test.

Answers

Place your answers in the right blanks or the corresponding bubbles on the answer sheet. Right answers in the wrong place earn no points. It's a good idea to check every five to ten questions to make sure you're in the right spot. That way you won't need much time to correct your answer sheet if you have made an error.

Choosing the Right Answers

Make sure you understand what the question is asking. If you're not sure of what's being asked, you'll never know whether you've chosen the right answer. So figure out what the question is asking. If the answer isn't readily apparent, look for clues in the answer choices. Notice the similarities and differences in the answer choices. Sometimes this helps to put the question in a new perspective and makes it easier to answer. If you're still not sure of the answer, use the process of elimination. First, eliminate any answer choices that are obviously wrong. Then reason your way through the remaining choices. You may be able to use relevant information from other parts of the test. If you can't eliminate any of the answer choices, you might be better off to skip the question and come back to it later. If you can't eliminate any answer choices to improve your odds when you come back later, then make a guess and move on.

If You're Penalized for Wrong Answers

You **must know** whether there's a penalty for wrong answers before you begin the test. If you don't, ask the proctor before the test begins. Whether you make a guess or not depends upon the penalty. Some standardized tests are scored in such a way that every wrong answer reduces your score by one fourth or one half of a point. Whatever the penalty, if you can eliminate enough choices to make the odds of answering the question better than the penalty for getting it wrong, make a guess.

Let's imagine you are taking a test in which each answer has four choices and you are penalized one fourth of a point for each wrong answer. If you have no clue and cannot eliminate any of the answer choices, you're better off leaving the question blank because the odds of answering correctly are one in four. This makes the penalty and the odds equal. However, if you can eliminate one of the choices, the odds are now in your favor. You have a one in three chance of answering the question correctly. Fortunately, few tests are scored using such elaborate means, but if your test is one of them, know the penalties and calculate your odds before you take a guess on a question.

If You Finish Early

Use any time you have left at the end of the test or test section to check your work. First, make certain you've put the answers in the right places. As you're doing this, make sure you've answered each question only once. Most standardized tests are scored in such a way that questions with more than one answer are marked wrong. If you've erased an answer, make sure you've done a good job. Check for stray marks on your answer sheet that could distort your score.

After you've checked for these obvious errors, take a second look at the more difficult questions. You've probably heard the folk wisdom about never changing an answer. If you have a good reason for thinking a response is wrong, change it.

VOCABULARY AND SPELLING QUESTIONS

As you approach the vocabulary or spelling portion of the test, some specific tactics will allow you to do your very best on those items.

- Let what you do know guide what you don't know. For example, use the familiar part of a word—a root, prefix, or suffix—to figure out the meaning of an unfamiliar word.
- Listen to the sound of a word in your head. If it doesn't sound familiar, try moving the accent around. You may be surprised at how good your instincts are for knowing when a word sounds right.
- Let the look of the word be your guide. If you train your eye to pick up on how words are supposed to look it will help you to make a good choice from among several options
- If you are allowed to mark on your paper, try writing the word in a margin. Sometimes the act of

writing it down will remind you of the definition or correct spelling.

- Read the context carefully. Often the sentence in which a word appears gives a clue to its meaning. Try using the word in a sentence of your own to see if it makes sense based on what you think is the definition.

THE DAYS BEFORE THE TEST

Physical Activity

Get some exercise in the days preceding the test. You'll send some extra oxygen to your brain and allow your thinking performance to peak on the day you take the test. Moderation is the key here. You don't want to exercise so much that you feel exhausted, but a little physical activity will invigorate your body and brain.

Balanced Diet

Like your body, your brain needs the proper nutrients to function well. Eat plenty of fruits and vegetables in the days before the test. Foods that are high in lecithin, such as fish and beans, are especially good choices. Lecithin is a mineral your brain needs for peak performance. You may even consider a visit to your local pharmacy to buy a bottle of lecithin tablets several weeks before your test.

Rest

Get plenty of sleep the nights before you take the test. Don't overdo it, though, or you'll make yourself as groggy as if you were overtired. Go to bed at a reasonable time, early enough to get the number of hours you need to function **effectively**. You'll feel relaxed and rested if you've gotten plenty of sleep in the days before you take the test.

Trial Run

At some point before you take the test, make a trial run to the testing center to see how long it takes. Rushing raises your emotional energy and lowers your intellectual capacity, so you want to allow plenty of time on test day to get to the testing center. Arriving 10–15 minutes early gives you time to relax and get situated.

TEST DAY

It's finally here, the day of the big test. Set your alarm early enough to allow plenty of time. Eat a good breakfast. Avoid anything that's really high in sugar, such as donuts. A sugar high turns into a sugar low after an hour or so. Cereal and toast, or anything with complex carbohydrates is a good choice. Eat only moderate amounts. You don't want to take a test feeling stuffed!

Pack a high energy snack to take with you. You may have a break sometime during the test when you can grab a quick snack. Bananas are great. They have a moderate amount of sugar and plenty of brain nutrients, such as potassium. Most proctors won't allow you to eat a snack while you're testing, but a peppermint shouldn't pose a problem. Peppermints are like smelling salts for your brain. If you lose your concentration or suffer from a momentary mental block, a peppermint can get you back on track. Don't forget the earlier advice about relaxing and taking a few deep breaths.

Leave early enough so you have plenty of time to get to the test center. Allow a few minutes for unexpected traffic. When you arrive, locate the restroom and use it. Few things interfere with concentration as much as a full bladder. Then find your seat and make sure it's comfortable. If it isn't, tell the proctor and ask to change to something you find more suitable.

Now relax and think positively! Before you know it the test will be over, and you'll walk away knowing you've done as well as you can.

AFTER THE TEST

Two things:

1. Plan a little celebration.
2. Go to it.

If you have something to look forward to after the test is over, you may find it easier to prepare well for the test and to keep moving during the test.

GOOD LUCK!

T he point of a book like this one is not so much to do the exercises as to gain some personal control over your own difficulties with spelling and vocabulary. Here are some ways of continuing to work toward that goal:

- If you have kept a list of words from other reading sources, ask someone to dictate your list, having you to spell and define each word.

- If you have not kept a list of words other than those from the lessons, ask someone to quiz you on the words lists in this book. Make index cards for the words you don't remember.

- Have someone quiz you on the list of problem spelling words that follows. Write the words you miss on index cards.

- Study all your index cards at odd moments throughout the day for one week. Arrange them in alphabetical order or organize them by category. Review five cards at a time. You could keep your words in a small note-book, but cards are better for several reasons:

  You can alphabetize and categorize words more quickly.

  It feels good to see the size of the deck get smaller week by week.

  Cards are portable. You can tuck them easily into your pocket or purse.

- At the end of a week ask someone to dictate all the words you studied. Eliminate the words you now spell correctly. Keep doing this each week until you have mastered all of the words in your deck.

- Keep your eyes, ears, and mind tuned in to words. Read the "On Language" page in the Sunday *New York Times* or books on language from the library or the bookstore. Make up your own exercises for the words you have learned. Listen carefully to the words in the world around you. There are more of them coming every day!

RECOMMENDED BOOKS

If you want further study in vocabulary and spelling, your local public library is a good place to start. Many libraries have Lifelong Learning Centers, where instructional books for adult learners like you can be found. Here are some titles you might seek out in the library or bookstore:

- *504 Absolutely Essential Words* by Murray Bromberg et al. (Barron's)
- *601 Words You Need to Know to Pass Your Exam* by Murray Bromberg and Julius Liebb (Barron's)
- *All About Words: An Adult Approach to Vocabulary Building* by Maxwell Nurnberg and Morris Rosenblum (Mentor Books)
- *Checklists for Vocabulary Study* by Richard Yorkey (Longman)
- *Contemporary Vocabulary* by Elliot Smith (St. Martin's)
- *The New York Times Captive Vocabulary* by Robert Greenman (New York Times)
- *Rapid Vocabulary Builder* by Norman Lewis (Berkeley)
- *Spelling Simplified* by Judi Kisselman-Turkel and Franklynn Peterson (Contemporary Books)
- *Word Watcher's Handbook* by Phyllis Martin (St. Martin's)

"TOUGHIE" LIST

Like most vocabulary and spelling books, this book includes a list of spelling demons, or words that are hard to spell for one reason or another. Unlike many such lists, this one is short enough to be manageable.

Group the words you want to learn and study only five or seven at a time. Repetition over time is what will help you to keep the words and their spellings in your head.

absence	guarantee	pursuit
address	harass	questionnaire
anxiety	hygienic	queue
arctic	initial	referred
beauty	jealous	scissors
bureau	jeopardy	receipt
cellular	justice	salary
circuit	leisure	schedule
colonel	lieutenant	secession
commitment	management	seize
cough	mnemonics	separate
courteous	ninety	solemn
definitely	necessary	souvenir
descend	noticeable	susceptible
dining	occurred	sympathy
discipline	official	tragedy
enthusiasm	omitted	transference
excellent	parallel	Tuesday
existence	perceive	uniform
fascinate	pneumonia	unique
feasible	principal	vague
flexible	psychology	weird

Most, if not all, of these words should go on your ongoing Keeper List—the one you will use to continue improving your vocabulary and spelling for the rest of your life.

LEARNINGEXPRESS

CALIFORNIA

_____ @ $35.00 California Police Officer
_____ @ $35.00 California State Police
_____ @ $35.00 California Corrections Officer
_____ @ $20.00 Law Enforcement Career Guide: California
_____ @ $35.00 California Firefighter
_____ @ $30.00 California Postal Worker

FLORIDA

_____ @ $35.00 Florida Police Officer
_____ @ $35.00 Florida Corrections Officer
_____ @ $20.00 Law Enforcement Career Guide: Florida
_____ @ $30.00 Florida Postal Worker

ILLINOIS

_____ @ $30.00 Chicago Police Officer Exam

MASSACHUSETTS

_____ @ $30.00 Massachusetts Police Officer
_____ @ $30.00 Massachusetts State Police Exam

NEW JERSEY

_____ @ $35.00 New Jersey Police Officer
_____ @ $30.00 New Jersey State Police
_____ @ $35.00 New Jersey Corrections Officer
_____ @ $20.00 Law Enforcement Career Guide: New Jersey
_____ @ $35.00 New Jersey Firefighter
_____ @ $30.00 New Jersey Postal Worker

NEW YORK

_____ @ $30.00 New York City/Nassau County Police Officer
_____ @ $30.00 Suffolk County Police Officer
_____ @ $30.00 New York State Police
_____ @ $30.00 New York Corrections Officer
_____ @ $20.00 Law Enforcement Career Guide: New York State
_____ @ $35.00 New York Firefighter
_____ @ $30.00 New York Postal Worker
_____ @ $25.00 New York City Sanitation Worker
_____ @ $25.00 New York City Bus Operator

TEXAS

_____ @ $35.00 Texas Police Officer
_____ @ $35.00 Texas State Police
_____ @ $35.00 Texas Corrections Officer
_____ @ $20.00 Law Enforcement Career Guide: Texas
_____ @ $35.00 Texas Firefighter
_____ @ $30.00 Texas Postal Worker

MIDWEST
(Illinois, Indiana, Michigan, Minnesota, Ohio, and Wisconsin)

_____ @ $30.00 Midwest Police Officer Exam
_____ @ $30.00 Midwest Firefighter Exam

The SOUTH
(Alabama, Arkansas, Georgia, Louisiana, Mississippi, North Carolina, South Carolina, and Virginia)

_____ @ $25.00 The South Police Officer Exam (Sept. 1997)
_____ @ $25.00 The South Firefighter Exam (Sept. 1997)

NATIONAL EDITIONS

_____ @ $14.00 Civil Service Career Starter
_____ @ $12.95 Bus Operator Exam National Edition (Sept. 1997)
_____ @ $12.95 Sanitation Worker Exam National Edition (Sept. 1997)
_____ @ $12.95 U. S. Postal Service 470 Battery Exam National Edition (Sept. 1997)
_____ @ $14.95 Armed Services Vocational Aptitude Battery [ASVAB] (Oct. 1997)

NATIONAL STANDARDS EXAMS

_____ @ $20.00 Home Health Aide National Standards Exam (Oct. 1997)
_____ @ $20.00 Nurse's Assistant National Standards Exam (Oct. 1997)
_____ @ $20.00 EMT–Basic National Standards Exam (Oct. 1997)

THE BASICS MADE EASY

_____ @ $12.00 Office Basics in 20 Minutes a Day
_____ @ $12.00 Job Hunting Basics in 20 Minutes a Day

To Order, Call Toll-Free: **1-888-551-JOBS, Dept. A040**

or mail this order form with your check/money order* to:

LearningExpress, Dept. A040, 20 Academy Street, Norwalk, CT 06850

Please allow at least 2-4 weeks for delivery. Prices subject to change without notice   *NY, MD, & CT residents add appropriate sales tax